Power-Up English
\<Pre-Intermediate\>

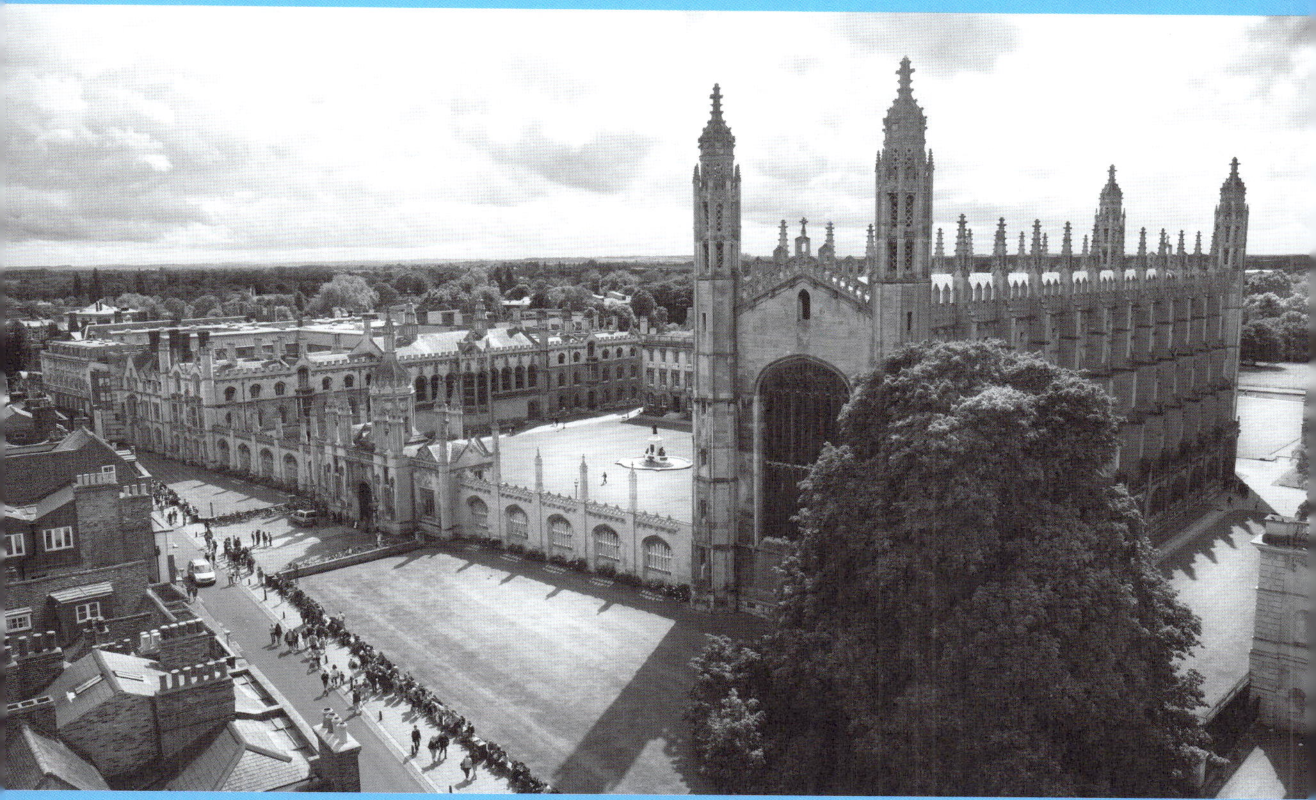

総合英語パワーアップ〈初級編〉

JACET リスニング研究会

このテキストの音声を無料で視聴（ストリーミング）・ダウンロードできます。自習用音声としてご活用ください。
以下のサイトにアクセスしてテキスト番号で検索してください。

https://nanun-do.com 　テキスト番号 [511639]

※ 無線 LAN（WiFi）に接続してのご利用を推奨いたします。

※ 音声ダウンロードは Zip ファイルでの提供になります。
　お使いの機器によっては別途ソフトウェア（アプリケーション）の導入が必要となります。

※ Power-Up English <Pre-Intermediate> 音声ダウンロードページは以下の QR コードからもご利用になれます。

Power-Up English <Pre-Intermediate>
総合英語パワーアップ〈初級編〉

by
JACET SIG on Listening

©2015 All Rights Reserved.

No part of this publication may be reproduced or transmitted in any form or by any means without permission from the authors and Nan'un-do Co., Ltd.

はじめに

　本書は，ロングセラーを続けているパワーアップシリーズの5作目にあたり，基礎的な英語の聴解力，読解力，文法力を効果的に向上させることを意図した総合英語教材です。*Power-Up English<Basic>* と *Power-Up English<Intermediate>* の中間に位置し，初級から中級への橋渡しとなるように幅広い習熟レベルの学習者を対象に作成されています。

　近年，グローバル社会にあって，英語のコミュニケーション能力が重視され，大学教育の場にも「使える英語」の習得を求める声が広がっています。英語が使えるようになるためには，第一に，話されたり書かれたりした英語を正確に理解する力が必要です。また，自分の言いたいことを話したり書いたりして発信するためには，正確な文法の知識を身につけることが不可欠です。本書は，学習者がこれまでに学んできた英語の聴解，読解，文法の基礎知識を有機的に結びつけ，しっかりと定着させることを目的としています。

　本書の特長は以下の3つです。1つ目は，題材としたトピックが豊富で多彩なことです。例えば，大学生活，恋愛，旅行，スポーツ，娯楽などの大学生にとって身近な話題から，現代の日本が抱える少子化や災害対策などの社会問題，さらには，芸術や文化や科学技術などの人類にとって普遍的なテーマまで，様々な分野の話題を採り上げています。2つ目は，各ユニットを構成するリスニング，リーディング，文法のセクションを1つのトピックで関連付けたことです。これによって，学習者は1つのトピックについて，インプットからアウトプットまでを体系的に学習することができます。3つ目は，英語の音声面を重視したことです。本書の音声部分は付属のCDを聞いて繰り返し学習できます。また，**Reading Section** には「**Read Aloud**」のコーナーを設け，短い文の英語らしい音読方法が全24ユニットを通して体験できるようにしています。さらに，巻末の「英語らしい音声をもとめて」では，各ユニットで学習した「**Listening Tips**」と関連させながら，英語の本格的な音声現象について詳しく解説しています。熟読すれば，英語らしい発音や音声現象のメカニズムについてのさらなる情報が得られ，将来的に英語の音声を学習するきっかけとなるでしょう。

　刊行にあたり，南雲堂編集部の加藤 敦氏，英文校閲などを担当していただきましたJim Knudsen氏に大変お世話になりました。ここに深く感謝の意を表します。

2014年8月
執筆者一同

本書の構成と学び方

> 本書は全24ユニットの構成で，通年用・半期用のどちらにも対応できるように心掛け，編集しました。各ユニットがそれぞれ独立していますので，半期で使用される場合には，学習者の専攻や関心などを考慮して学習するユニットを選択することも可能です。各ユニットは **Listening Section**（1ページ），**Reading Section**（2ページ），**Grammar Section**（1ページ）の3セクションから成り立ち，各セクションとも，*Exercise* に至るまで，使用語句や表現がトピックと関連性を持つように配慮しました。英語のアウトプットに役立つことを意図しています。さらに，各ユニットのフォーマットを統一したことで，学習計画が立てやすく，授業運営も円滑に進められます。各セクションの構成と内容は次の通りです。

Listening Section

◆ *Listening Tips* :
英語の音声の聞き取りを助けるヒントを用例付きで簡潔に紹介しています。文の強勢やポーズなどの基本的なルールから，消える音，つながる音，音の同化などの音声変化，また，リスニングの際に重要である否定形や短縮形の聞き取り，さらには，数量表現の聞き取りやアメリカ英語の特徴についても解説しています。全ユニットを通して学べば，英語のリスニングについてのコツが得られ，リスニング力の向上に役立ちます。

◆ *Exercise 1* :
「絵」に関わる，4つの短い描写文を聞き，「絵」について正しく叙述している文を1つ選ぶ問題です。TOEICのPart Iに準じた問題です。

◆ *Exercise 2* :
発話とそれに対する3つの応答を聞き，発話に対する最もふさわしい応答を1つ選ぶ問題です。TOEICのPart IIに対応した問題です。

◆ *Exercise 3* :
100語程度の英文を聞き，あらかじめテキストに印刷された2つの設問に答える問題です。TOEICのPart IIIおよびPart IVに相当します。出題形式に変化を持たせるために，奇数ユニットはダイアローグ形式，偶数ユニットはモノローグ形式にしてあります。

Reading Section

◆ *Words & Phrases* :
Reading Passage に現れる語句とそれに一致する日本語訳を選択する問題です。本文の理解にとって重要な語句の意味をあらかじめ確認することができます。

◆ *Reading Passage* :
各ユニットのトピックに関連した題材を取り上げて，約250語～300語で書かれた英文です。内容理解の助けとなる注釈を英文の下に設け，固有名詞，語句などの補足説明を行っています。

◆ *Exercise 1* :
空所補充形式で本文の内容理解を確認する問題です。全ユニットを通して，設問の中に，Main Ideaを問う問題と文中の語句の意味を問う問題を1題ずつ設けています。

◆ *Exercise 2* :
　本文の内容について書かれた英文の真偽を問う問題です。*Reading Passage* で述べられた内容についての細かい理解を確認することができます。

◆ **Read Aloud** :
　Reading Passage から主として抜粋した英文の音読練習をします。強勢が置かれる単語やポーズの位置に注意して，英語独特のリズムを意識しながら音読してください。実際に英語らしい発音を体験することが，ひいてはリスニング力の向上にも繋がります。独自の音読にとどめず，ペアやグループで音読し合って，お互いにコメントするのもよいことでしょう。ぜひ，繰り返し練習することをお勧めします。

◆ **Information for the Topic** :
　Reading Passage で取り上げたトピックに関して，興味を喚起させるような情報を盛り込んでいます。トピックについてさらに知識を広げ，考察を深めてください。

Grammar Section
◆ *Grammar Points* :
　英語のコミュニケーションに必要な基本的な文法項目を，用例付きで簡潔にまとめています。例文は初級者にも分かりやすいように，なるべく典型的なものを選んでいます。また，文法事項が視覚的に整理できるように，表形式を使ってレイアウトにも工夫を凝らしています。問題を解く前に一読すれば，短時間で基本的な文法事項を一通り学習することができます。

◆ *Exercise 1* :
　空所に入る適切な語句を選択肢の中から選ぶ問題です。*Grammar Points* で取り扱った文法事項の理解を確認することができます。

◆ *Exercise 2* :
　日本語訳に合うように空所に適切な語句を補充する問題です。和文英訳の前段階として学習者のアウトプット能力を向上させます。

◆ *Exercise 3* :
　語句を並べ替えて英文を完成させる問題です。*Grammar Points* で学習した文法項目を総括して英作文能力の基礎を養成します。

Appendix
◆「英語らしい音声をもとめて」:
　各ユニットの *Listening Tips* で扱った英語特有の音声現象について，音声学的な立場から詳しく解説しています。また，リスニング力の向上には英語らしい発音ができることが重要ですので，英文の発音の仕方についての情報も含めています。多彩な例を盛り込み，専門用語を使わずに平易な文章で解説するように心掛けました。*Listening Tips* で習得した知識を定着させるために授業と並行して読んだり，復習のために全ユニットを学習し終えた段階で読んだりして，大いに活用してください。

CONTENTS

Unit 1 **College Life (I)** ● **Welcome to College**「大学へようこそ」
文の強勢とポーズ　品詞 ……………………………………… 9

Unit 2 **College Life (II)** ● **Course Registration**「履修登録」
英語のリズム　自動詞・他動詞 ……………………………… 13

Unit 3 **Hobbies** ● **Do It Yourself**「自分自身でやってみよう」
イントネーション　5文型 …………………………………… 17

Unit 4 **Romance** ● **The Guardian of Love**「愛の守護聖人」
消える音Ⅰ　現在形・過去形 ………………………………… 21

Unit 5 **Transportation** ● **Low-Cost Carriers**「格安航空会社」
消える音Ⅱ　未来を表す表現 ………………………………… 25

Unit 6 **Business** ● **An Indian Restaurateur**「インド料理店の経営者」
消える音Ⅲ　進行形 …………………………………………… 29

Unit 7 **Society** ● **Global Self-Help Revolution**「グローバル自立支援革命」
つながる音Ⅰ　完了形 ………………………………………… 33

Unit 8 **Health** ● **Achilles Tendon Rupture**「アキレス腱断裂」
つながる音Ⅱ　助動詞 ………………………………………… 37

Unit 9 **The Environment** ● **Aluminum-can Recycling**「アルミ缶リサイクル」
つながる音Ⅲ　受動態 ………………………………………… 41

Unit 10 **Medicine** ● **Alternative Medicine**「代替医療」
音の同化Ⅰ　不定詞 …………………………………………… 45

Unit 11 **Finance** ● **Two Big Players**「金融界の二大巨頭」
音の同化Ⅱ　分詞 ……………………………………………… 49

Unit 12 **Shopping** ● **Smart Shopping**「スマート・ショッピング」
弱形と強形　動名詞 …………………………………………… 53

Unit	Topic	Title	Subtopics	Page
Unit 13	Careers	Job Hunting「就職活動」	notの短縮形 ❖ 形容詞・副詞	57
Unit 14	Art	The Shadow of a Great Artist「偉大な芸術家の苦悩」	be動詞・助動詞の短縮形 ❖ 名詞・代名詞	61
Unit 15	Culture	Everyday Japan and "Matsuri" Japan「日本の日常と祭りのギャップ」	疑問詞の聞き取り ❖ 前置詞	65
Unit 16	Population	The Declining Birthrate「深刻な少子化」	展開を予測しながら聞く ❖ 接続詞	69
Unit 17	Disasters	Narrow Escape「危機一髪」	無声音化・有声音化 ❖ いろいろな否定	73
Unit 18	Travel	Invitation to Hokkaido「北海道への招待」	まぎらわしい音 ❖ 名詞構文・無生物主語構文	77
Unit 19	Sports	The World's Most Popular Sport?「世界一人気のスポーツは？」	数量表現Ⅰ ❖ 比較表現Ⅰ：原級・比較級・最上級	81
Unit 20	Life	Quality of Life「生活の質」	数量表現Ⅱ ❖ 比較表現Ⅱ：いろいろな比較表現	85
Unit 21	Entertainment	Television Prime Time「TVのプライムタイム」	知っているつもりの英語 ❖ 関係詞Ⅰ：関係代名詞	89
Unit 22	Language	Loanwords in Japanese「日本語における借用語」	通じているつもりの英語 ❖ 関係詞Ⅱ：関係副詞	93
Unit 23	Science	The Goal of Science「科学の目的」	アメリカ英語の特徴Ⅰ ❖ 仮定法Ⅰ：仮定法過去・仮定法過去完了	97
Unit 24	Technology	A Language Robot「言語ロボット」	アメリカ英語の特徴Ⅱ ❖ 仮定法Ⅱ：いろいろな仮定表現	101
Appendix		英語らしい音声をもとめて		106

Power-Up English
<Pre-Intermediate>

Unit 1　College Life (I)

Listening Section

Listening Tips

文の強勢とポーズ —強く発音されるところと短く間を空けるところはどこ？—

ふつう英語では内容語(動詞[be 動詞は除く]，名詞，形容詞，副詞，疑問詞，感嘆詞など)は強く発音され，機能語(be 動詞，冠詞，代名詞，助動詞，前置詞，接続詞など)は弱く発音されます。他方，文中において，ふつうポーズを置くところは，句や節の切れ目や接続詞の前などです。例えば，次の例では，●印が強く発音されるところ，／印がポーズを置くところです。

I graduated from high school in March ／ and I am a college student now.

Exercise 1 Listen to the CD and choose the statement that best describes the picture.

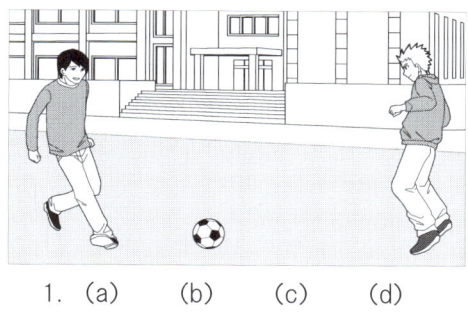

1. (a)　(b)　(c)　(d)　　　　2. (a)　(b)　(c)　(d)

Exercise 2 Listen to the CD and choose the best response.

1. (a)　(b)　(c)　　　　　　2. (a)　(b)　(c)
3. (a)　(b)　(c)　　　　　　4. (a)　(b)	(c)

Exercise 3 Listen to the CD and answer the questions.

1. Where is Masao's apartment?
   (a) On campus
   (b) Near the campus
   (c) On a large hill with a view of the campus
   (d) About ten minutes' walk from Michiko's house

2. Which of the following statements is true?
   (a) Masao just moved in his new apartment last month.
   (b) Michiko doesn't have to worry about being late for school anymore.
   (c) Michiko agreed to help Masao buy some daily necessities.
   (d) A new supermarket is going to open near the college soon.

Unit 1

Reading Section
Welcome to College

Words & Phrases — 次の語句の意味を選びなさい。

1. adjustment (　)　2. expectation (　)　3. critical (　)　4. passive (　)
5. independence (　)　6. responsibility (　)　7. priority (　)
8. concentrate (　)　9. relaxation (　)　10. sum up (　)

　　(a) 重要な　　(b) 責任　　(c) 要約する　　(d) 受動的な　　(e) 自立
　　(f) 期待　　(g) 気晴らし　　(h) 適応　　(i) 優先　　(j) 集中する

次の文を読んで，後の設問に答えなさい。

Reading Passage

　Welcome to college. Your first semester here might be a little difficult and stressful because of the many adjustments you will have to make. But it will also be a time filled with great expectations and wonderful discoveries. Let me tell you a little about what lies ahead and how you can be sure to have a successful college career.

　In class, active participation is critical. You don't want to be a passive learner who just sits and listens to the teacher. Instead, you should actively express your opinions, ask questions, and explain your ideas.

　You also need to learn to take care of things on your own. You will have a lot more freedom to make your own choices and decisions than when you were in high school. But be careful, because such an increase in independence also means an increase in responsibility.

　You should develop good study habits and make it a top priority to attend all your classes. This will enable you to concentrate on what you are studying and to do everything expected of you. At the same time, you should also take part in school events—concerts, contests, meetings, festivals, and so on. This will give you the opportunity to make friends with other students, and it can also be a form of relaxation.

　To sum up, college is indeed the time of life when you can enjoy many different things. But it's also a period of preparation for your future dreams. Always keep in mind that your main task is to study hard. Good luck!

(260 words)

on your own　独力で　　a form of ~　ある種の～

College Life (I)

Exercise 1 （　）内に入る最も適切な語句を選び，文を完成させなさい。

1. This message is most likely given by a (　　).
   (a) high school principal　　　(b) college president
   (c) student's parent　　　　　(d) club manager
2. The word *career* in line 5 means (　　).
   (a) carriage　　(b) education　　(c) life　　(d) future
3. College students are expected to deal with things (　　).
   (a) without complaining　　　(b) with their new friends
   (c) for themselves　　　　　　(d) against their will
4. An increase in independence should come with an increase in (　　).
   (a) responsibility　(b) freedom　(c) friendship　(d) wealth
5. College is a place where students should study hard to (　　) their dreams for the future.
   (a) give up　　(b) spoil　　(c) realize　　(d) recognize

Exercise 2　次の各文が本文の内容に合っていればT(True)，合っていなければF(False)を書きなさい。

_____ 1. College students are expected to be quiet learners who just sit and listen in class.
_____ 2. College students will enjoy less freedom to make their own choices and decisions than when they were in high school.
_____ 3. Regular attendance of all the classes will help the students concentrate on what they are studying.
_____ 4. Campus festivals can give students a chance to make friends with other students.
_____ 5. College life is a period when students have a lot of chances to experience various things.

Read Aloud　強く発音するところ（7か所）の○を黒く塗りつぶし，ポーズを置くところ（1か所）に／を書き入れ，CDを聞いて音読しなさい。　*T*-CD 1-8

You should develop good study habits and attend all your classes.
　○　　　　○　　　　　○　　　　○　　　　○　　　　○　　　○　　　○　　　○　　　○　　　○

ℹ Information for the Topic

大学は多すぎるか？

　日本の大学は多すぎるのでしょうか。確かに全国の大学数は，戦後間もないころの201校（1950年度）から，約450校（1985年度）を経て現在781校（2014年度）にまで急増しています。四年制大学への進学率も過去最高の51.5％（2014年度）となり，世界でトップクラスの高等教育大国ですが，大学進学率から判断する限り，オーストラリア96％，ニュージーランド76％，ロシア72％，韓国71％，アメリカ65％，イギリス63％など，日本より高い国もあって，「大学の淘汰を進めるよりもむしろ増やして競争を促すべき」との声も聞かれます。

Unit 1

Grammar Section
品　詞

Grammar Points

▶英語の語は，文中での働きによって 8 つの品詞に分類されます。

名　詞	人または事物の名称や概念を表す語	John, school, holiday, car
代名詞	名詞の代わりをする語	I, you, this, mine, himself
形容詞	名詞や代名詞を修飾する語	tall, dark, handsome, nice
副　詞	動詞，形容詞，副詞を修飾する語	soon, very, only, just, almost
動　詞	主語の動作や状態を表す語	be, come, have, give, speak
前置詞	名詞や代名詞の前に置いて，他の語との関係を示す語	by, in, from, through, into
接続詞	語と語，句と句，節と節を結びつける語	and, but, if, though, because
間投詞	文中のいずれの語とも関係がなく，喜怒哀楽の感情を表したり，呼びかけたりする語	oh, wow, oops, aha, ugh, eh, hum, whew, hey

Exercise 1　(　) 内に入る最も適切な語句を選びなさい。

1. You should be (quiet / quietly) in the library.
2. "(Father / My father), is it all right if I work a part-time job?"　"No way!"
3. She was on (friend / friendly) terms with her classmates.
4. He enjoyed talking with his friends (during / while) lunch.

Exercise 2　日本語に合うように (　) 内に適切な語を書き入れなさい。

1. I would like to (　　　　) for a scholarship next year.
   （来年，奨学金に応募したい）
2. Try not to be (　　　　) for class.（授業に遅れないようにしなさい）
3. Didn't we discuss this problem in class (　　　　)?
   （以前，授業でこの問題について話し合いませんでしたか）
4. He rented an apartment (　　　　) the college to cut his commuting time.
   （彼は通学時間節約のため，大学の近くに部屋を借りた）

Exercise 3　(　) 内の語を並べかえて英文を完成させなさい。

1. There (tower / beside / a / the / clock / is / tall) library.

2. Some (a / students / on / tent / up / international / put) the beach.

3. You (start / your / before / hunting / to / have / job) your senior year.

Unit 2　College Life (II)

Listening Section

---**Listening Tips**---

英語のリズム　―文単位での強勢はどうなる？―

英語のリズムは，強勢が置かれ強く聞こえる音節（●で表示）と，その谷間の弱く聞こえる音節（•で表示）から構成されています。強勢が時間的にほぼ等間隔で現れるリズムを保持する傾向があるため，谷間の弱音節は音節数が多くなるほど速く，圧縮したように聞こえます。

College students visit the website to register for the courses.
●　　•　●　•　　•　●　•　　•　●　•　•　　●　•

Exercise 1　Listen to the CD and choose the statement that best describes the picture.

1. (a)　(b)　(c)　(d)　　2. (a)　(b)　(c)　(d)

Exercise 2　Listen to the CD and choose the best response.

1. (a)　(b)　(c)　　　　2. (a)　(b)　(c)
3. (a)　(b)　(c)　　　　4. (a)　(b)　(c)

Exercise 3　Listen to the CD and answer the questions.

1. Who most likely are the listeners?
   (a) Students who want to take Professor Scott's course
   (b) Students who have experienced culture shock
   (c) Students who took part in the Study-Abroad program last year
   (d) Students who are interested in studying overseas

2. Which of the following statements is true?
   (a) Professor Scott will talk about how to get over culture shock.
   (b) The speaker hopes the listeners will apply for the Study-Abroad Program.
   (c) Professor Scott will give students some tips on how to improve their TOEFL scores.
   (d) The listeners will take the TOEFL test during the last session.

Unit 2

Reading Section
Course Registration

Words & Phrases 次の語句の意味を選びなさい。

1. registration ( ) 2. sign up ( ) 3. grading ( ) 4. handout ( )
5. introductory ( ) 6. interview ( ) 7. intermediate ( )
8. downloadable ( ) 9. presentation ( ) 10. upper-intermediate ( )

(a) ダウンロード可能な (b) 成績 (c) 口頭発表 (d) 申し込む (e) 中上級の
(f) 登録 (g) 面接 (h) 入門の (i) 中級の (j) 配布物

次の文を読んで，後の設問に答えなさい。

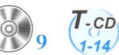

Reading Passage

During "Registration," you must read syllabuses or course descriptions to help you decide which courses to take. When you sign up, always take the teacher, textbook, course requirements, and grading system into consideration. Suppose you want to take an English conversation course. Which one of these courses would interest you?

Oral English Communication I Dr. Peter Cruise Textbook: handouts

In this introductory class, students will talk about everyday topics such as hobbies, interests, part-time jobs, and student life, and will learn basic conversational phrases through pair and group work. Active participation is encouraged. Class meets twice a week. Students will take a mid-term test (a group interview) and a final test (an individual interview).

Oral English Communication II Dr. Paul Churchill Textbook: TBA

This is an intermediate-level course. Students must have completed Oral English Communication I. The course aims to help students improve their listening and speaking skills. In each class, after viewing DVD clips or surfing the Internet, students will discuss a variety of topics, including sports, health, travel, and social problems. Some of the learning materials are downloadable. At the end of the course, students will take an oral interview test and give a final presentation.

Business Communication I Dr. Jane Carnegie Textbook: *Introductory Business*

This course is an upper-intermediate level course, with a focus on business English. Topics cover job hunting, telephone conversations, business meetings, overseas business trips, etc. Students will learn basic business-related vocabulary and phrases. As homework assignments, students are occasionally required to read and write business letters. Grading is based on homework assignments, quizzes, and a final written and oral test.

(267 words)

mid-term test 中間テスト   final test 期末テスト   TBA = To Be Announced   learning material 教材

College Life (II)

Exercise 1 （　）内に入る最も適切な語句を選び，文を完成させなさい。

1. Syllabuses or course (　　) help students decide which courses to sign up for.
   (a) descriptions　(b) evaluations　(c) registrations　(d) reviews

2. The word *requirements* in line 3 means what students (　　).
   (a) like to do　(b) hate to do　(c) need to do　(d) want to do

3. Students who take Oral English Communication I will mainly discuss (　　).
   (a) business matters　　(b) everyday topics
   (c) social problems　　(d) any topics that the participants choose

4. In Oral English Communication II, students are supposed to (　　) after viewing DVD clips.
   (a) surf the Internet　　(b) engage in discussion
   (c) give a presentation　(d) take a test

5. Students need to (　　) in Business Communication I.
   (a) download learning materials　(b) hand in a research paper
   (c) search the Internet　　　　 (d) write business letters

Exercise 2 次の各文が本文の内容に合っていればT(True)，合っていなければF(False)を書きなさい。

_____ 1. Before taking Oral English Communication II, students need to take Oral English Communication I.
_____ 2. Dr. Churchill uses audiovisual materials in his class.
_____ 3. Dr. Carnegie gives a test in the middle of the course.
_____ 4. Students need to buy textbooks for all of the courses.
_____ 5. Students need to attend classes twice a week in all of the courses.

Read Aloud　強く発音するところ（7か所）の○を黒く塗りつぶし，ポーズを置くところ（1か所）に／を書き入れ，CDを聞いて音読しなさい。

At the end of the course, students will take an oral interview test.
○　○○　○　　○　　○　　　○　　　　○　○　○　○　　　　○

ℹ Information for the Topic

留学するには？

　多くの大学では，website（ホームページ）で大学の概要，特色，学部・学科，教員，施設などの様々な情報を紹介しています。さらに，将来の留学生（prospective international students）向けの情報も提供しています。もし留学したいと思ったら，入学条件（admission requirements）を入念にチェックしましょう。個人的な質問がある場合は，まず問い合わせる前に「よくある質問（FAQ）」を確認してみましょう。それでも解決しない場合は，担当窓口に質問することが大切です。

Unit 2

Grammar Section
自動詞・他動詞

Grammar Points

▶ 英語の動詞は，目的語の有無によって自動詞と他動詞の2種類に分かれます。

自動詞	動詞の直後に目的語が必要でない動詞	The train always **arrives** on time.
他動詞	動詞の直後に目的語を必要とする動詞	We **learn** many subjects in English.

✍ 自動詞と間違えやすい他動詞：accompany, discuss, enjoy, mention, resemble
✍ 他動詞と間違えやすい自動詞：apologize, disagree, listen, matter

▶ 自動詞と他動詞の両方の用法があっても，自動詞と他動詞で意味が異なる動詞もあります。
I **run**.／I will **run** in the election. 自「走る／出馬する」I **run** a company. 他「〜を経営する」
I **called** on my cousin at five. 自「訪れる」I **called** my cousin at five. 他「〜に電話する」

▶ 紛らわしい自動詞・他動詞に注意しましょう。
lie 自「横たわる」lay 他「〜を置く」／ rise 自「上がる」raise 他「〜を上げる」

Exercise 1　(　) 内に入る最も適切な語句を選びなさい。

1. (Listen / Listen to) the listening comprehension CD every day.

2. A friend of mine (approached / approached to) me to say, "Hello."

3. The teacher (said / told) the students that his lecture would be canceled.

4. I (enjoyed / enjoyed myself) a lot at the party.

Exercise 2　日本語に合うように (　) 内に適切な語を書き入れなさい。

1. Let me (　　　　　) the key points of my presentation.
   （私のプレゼンテーションの重要点について言及させてください）

2. Please (　　　　　) your hand if you have any questions.
   （何か質問があれば挙手してください）

3. Because I was late for class, I (　　　　　) to my teacher.
   （授業に遅れたので，先生に謝った）

4. I (　　　　　) for Student Council President.（生徒会長に立候補した）

Exercise 3　(　) 内の語を並べかえて英文を完成させなさい。

1. If (you / find / building, / you'll / enter / the) the administration office just inside the front door on your right.

2. I am going to (lecture / psychology / attend / afternoon / this / on / the).

3. With (reading / partner, / discuss / your / effective / strategies / that / the) you use.

Unit 3　Hobbies

Listening Section

> **Listening Tips**
>
> イントネーション　—声の上がり，下がりはどうなる？—
>
> 　英語の文は，声の上がり，下がりによって，話者の感情や意図を表現します。イントネーションには，下降調，上昇調，水平調の3つの基本型があります。
>
> ［下降調］　My hobby is reading detective fiction. (↘)　　（平叙文）
> 　　　　　What is your hobby? (↘)　　　　　　　　　　（疑問詞のある疑問文）
> ［上昇調］　Do you have any hobbies? (↗)　　　　　　　　（疑問詞のない疑問文）
> ［水平調］　My hobby is reading detective fiction (→) and yours is fishing.（未完結の文）

Exercise 1　Listen to the CD and choose the statement that best describes the picture.

1.　(a)　　(b)　　(c)　　(d)　　　2.　(a)　　(b)　　(c)　　(d)

Exercise 2　Listen to the CD and choose the best response.

1.　(a)　(b)　(c)　　　　2.　(a)　(b)　(c)
3.　(a)　(b)　(c)　　　　4.　(a)　(b)　(c)

Exercise 3　Listen to the CD and answer the questions.

1. What is necessary to make sure you get a good harvest?
　(a) Buying plants only at a garden center store
　(b) Choosing healthy vegetables
　(c) Keeping vegetables out of the wind and rain
　(d) Protecting vegetables from disease or insects

2. Which of the following statements is true?
　(a) One of Yoshiko's hobbies is growing flowers.
　(b) It takes a few months to harvest crops from young plants.
　(c) Home-grown vegetables don't need watering every day.
　(d) Beginners shouldn't try to grow tomatoes.

● 17

Unit 3

Reading Section

Do It Yourself

Words & Phrases 次の語句の意味を選びなさい。

1. fix ( ) 2. flat ( ) 3. leak ( ) 4. concept ( )
5. reconstruction ( ) 6. productive ( ) 7. profit ( )
8. tip ( ) 9. ensure ( ) 10. halfway ( )

(a) 確実にする (b) 生産的な (c) 復興 (d) 実益 (e) パンクした
(f) 着想 (g) 途中で (h) 秘訣 (i) 修繕する (j) 水漏れがする

次の文を読んで，後の設問に答えなさい。

Reading Passage

　Have you ever made a bookshelf for your room? Have you ever painted a dog house or fixed a flat bicycle tire? Have you ever stopped a faucet from leaking? Performing these tasks on your own without calling in a paid expert is the basis of "Do it yourself."

5　The "Do it yourself," or DIY, idea was born in Britain in 1945, just after World War II. In London, which had almost been completely destroyed by German aerial bombing, people started a movement to rebuild the city. Londoners' slogan, "Do it yourself," immediately spread throughout Europe and then to the US, where the concept changed from "reconstruction" to "productive activity for a comfortable

10　life." Many Americans took up DIY tasks as a hobby. In the early 1970s, DIY for pleasure and profit was welcomed in Japan, too. Since then, the number of people who engage in DIY has steadily grown. Today, DIY corners in home-improvement centers across the country are almost always crowded with DIY fans.

　Why don't you join a DIY group? All it takes is a bit of know-how, a little courage,

15　and some practice, and you'll become a successful do-it-yourselfer in no time. It will not only be fun, but also give you a great sense of achievement.

　The following are some easy tips to ensure DIY success.

・Learn all you can about your chosen project.
・Gather your tools and learn how to use them correctly.

20　・Work at your own pace. Don't try to do too much too quickly.
・Start with a simpler project so you don't give up halfway.

(263 words)

Do It Yourself 自らの手でやろう　faucet 蛇口　DIY do it yourself の頭字語　aerial bombing 空爆
movement（社会的）運動　Londoner ロンドン市民　home-improvement center ホームセンター
do-it-yourselfer DIY 愛好家　in no time たちどころに　a sense of achievement 達成感

18

 Hobbies

Exercise 1 (　　) 内に入る最も適切な語句を選び，文を完成させなさい。

1. This passage focuses mainly on the history of DIY and some (　　) for how to achieve DIY success.
   (a) advice　　　(b) values　　　(c) examples　　　(d) problems
2. Performing DIY tasks on your own is the basic (　　) of "Do it yourself."
   (a) skill　　　(b) result　　　(c) idea　　　(d) profit
3. Londoners' DIY slogan immediately spread all over (　　).
   (a) the U.S. and to Japan　　　(b) Britain and to the U.S.
   (c) Britain and to Germany　　　(d) Europe and to the U.S.
4. The word *steadily* in line 12 means (　　).
   (a) at a speed that doesn't change very much　(b) at a speed that often changes
   (c) at a slow speed　　　(d) at a high speed
5. You should (　　) in order not to give up in the middle of work.
   (a) learn all you can　　　(b) work at your own pace
   (c) start with a simpler project　　　(d) gather your tools

Exercise 2　次の各文が本文の内容に合っていればT(True), 合っていなければF(False)を書きなさい。

_____ 1. The German army almost destroyed London in ground attacks during World War II.
_____ 2. After the war, people in London started a movement with the slogan "productive activity for a comfortable life."
_____ 3. In the early 1970s, Japanese people welcomed DIY for pleasure but not for profit.
_____ 4. You need some special knowledge and tools to become a successful do-it-yourselfer.
_____ 5. You should finish projects as quickly as you can so you don't become bored.

Read Aloud　強く発音するところ(6か所)の○を黒く塗りつぶし，ポーズを置くところ(2か所)に／を書き入れ，CDを聞いて音読しなさい。

In London people started a movement to rebuild the city.
○　○　　　○　　○　　○　　　　○　○　　○　○

i Information for the Topic

DIY(Do It Yourself)の概念
　直訳すれば，「自分自身でそれをやりなさい」となりますが，「自分自身でやる」という意味です。本棚を作ったり，水道の水漏れを直すなど，生活空間をより快適にするため，専門家や業者などに依頼せず，自分で作ったり，修理できるものは自分の手でやりましょうという概念を指します。DIYのメリットとして，自分で作ったり修理した方が安く済むことや，既製品にはない自分に合ったものが作られることが考えられますが，何よりも，他に代え難い達成感や充実感が得られるのが魅力です。

Unit 3

Grammar Section
5 文 型

Grammar Points

▶英語の文は動詞を中心に成り立ち，構成要素の組み合わせによって5つの文型に分けられます。

第1文型	主語＋動詞 ＜S＋V＞ SとVのほかに修飾語句を伴うことが多い。	Mary smiled.
第2文型	主語＋動詞＋補語 ＜S＋V＋C＞ Cは名詞もしくは形容詞。S＝Cの関係が成り立つ。	She was cute.
第3文型	主語＋動詞＋目的語 ＜S＋V＋O＞ Oは名詞もしくは代名詞など。	John liked her.
第4文型	主語＋動詞＋目的語$_1$＋目的語$_2$ ＜S＋V＋O$_1$＋O$_2$＞ O$_1$は「人」，O$_2$は「物」。第3文型に書き換え可能。	He gave her a doll.
第5文型	主語＋動詞＋目的語＋補語 ＜S＋V＋O＋C＞ O＝Cの関係が成り立つ。	He made her happy.

Exercise 1　（　）内に入る最も適切な語句を選びなさい。

1. Peter made a doghouse (to / for) his dog.
2. She explained (us her reading plan / her reading plan to us).
3. Who did you give your treasured memorial (stamp collection / stamp collection to)?
4. I hear you are going to show your paintings in the exhibition. I (hope / wish) you good luck.

Exercise 2　日本語に合うように（　）内に適切な語を書き入れなさい。

1. Would you (　　　　)(　　　　) a taxi to take me to the concert hall?
 （コンサートホールへ行くのに，タクシーを呼んでいただけますか）
2. My sister is very (　　　　)(　　　　) arranging flowers.
 （妹は生け花が大好きです）
3. My grandfather (　　　　)(　　　　) a large collection of antiques.
 （祖父は私たちに多大の骨董収集品を残してくれた）
4. While rock-climbing, he (　　　　)(　　　　) the pool below a waterfall.
 （ロッククライミングの最中に，彼は滝壺に落ちました）

Exercise 3　（　）内の語を並べかえて英文を完成させなさい。

1. The coat my mother made me (warm / cold / will / in / me / keep) weather.

2. "Who (the / talking / you / on / were / with) street?" "She's my dance instructor."

3. She likes (tales / children / read / her / to / fairy) at bedtime.

Unit 4 Romance

Listening Section

Listening Tips

消える音 I　―**Very good.** はどう聞こえる？―

自然な会話では，文が [p][t][k][b][d][g] などの子音で終わるとき，その音がはっきりと聞こえないことがあります。例えば，Very good. の good の部分は「グッド」ではなく「グー」となり，[d] の音が聞こえにくくなることがあります。

1. That's good.　　　2. What a cute dog!　　　3. Don't stop!
4. What?　　　　　　5. Hi, Bob.　　　　　　　6. Look!

Exercise 1　Listen to the CD and choose the statement that best describes the picture.

1. (a)　(b)　(c)　(d)　　　2. (a)　(b)　(c)　(d)

Exercise 2　Listen to the CD and choose the best response.

1. (a)　(b)　(c)　　　　　2. (a)　(b)　(c)
3. (a)　(b)　(c)　　　　　4. (a)　(b)　(c)

Exercise 3　Listen to the CD and answer the questions.

1. What is the main topic of the talk?
   (a) How to select lovely stationery
   (b) How to choose romantic music
   (c) How to write a letter for a special purpose
   (d) How to address an envelope and post a letter

2. What should a love-letter writer NOT do?
   (a) Listen to romantic music while writing the letter
   (b) Write the letter in a private place
   (c) Spray the letter lightly with perfume
   (d) Draft the letter quickly and copy it right away

Unit 4

Reading Section
The Guardian of Love

Words & Phrases 次の語句の意味を選びなさい。

1. concern ( ) 2. suicide ( ) 3. unite ( ) 4. tragic ( )
5. honor ( ) 6. curious ( ) 7. exist ( )
8. reply ( ) 9. fictional ( ) 10. sacred ( )

(a) 存在する (b) 自殺 (c) 悲劇の (d) 架空の (e) 返事
(f) 団結させる (g) 聖なる (h) 関心 (i) 奇妙な (j) 尊敬する

次の文を読んで，後の設問に答えなさい。

Reading Passage

　Love is one of life's greatest concerns for men and women, young and old. Stories of romance have been told from the beginning of human history. It is not too much to say that William Shakespeare's *Romeo and Juliet* is the most popular love story in world literature. It is a tragedy based on an Italian folk story about two young lovers whose families are in deep conflict. It ends with the lovers' double suicide, and their deaths shock the two quarreling families into uniting.

　Many people regard this romantic tale as a symbol of love that does not go as the lovers desired. In particular, the tragic heroine, Juliet, is honored as a guardian of lovers. As a result, a curious thing has happened in Verona, where Shakespeare set the story. Though Juliet never really existed, people with love troubles still like to go to Verona and visit the places that appear in the story. Some leave notes at the house and tomb where, according to the story, Juliet lived and was buried. Even more curious, couples from around the world write letters to Juliet asking her advice. An organization called "Juliet's Club" was set up by volunteer "secretaries" who write replies to the letters in Juliet's name.

　Today, Juliet's House, with its famous balcony, is a popular sightseeing spot for tourists. Many believe that touching the right breast of the bronze statue of Juliet in the courtyard will bring them luck in love. It doesn't matter that Juliet is a fictional character. Juliet's House is a sacred place for people who are trying to find true love.

(269 words)

it is not too much to say that ~ ～と言っても過言ではない　　William Shakespeare ウィリアム・シェイクスピア (1564-1616) イギリスの劇作家　　based on ~ ～に基づいている　　quarreling 言い争ってばかりの　　courtyard 中庭　　it doesn't matter that ~ たとえ～でも問題ない

Exercise 1 （　）内に入る最も適切な語句を選び，文を完成させなさい。

1. This passage focuses mainly on (　　) of *Romeo and Juliet*.
   (a) the writer　　(b) the hero　　(c) the heroine　　(d) the stage
2. *Romeo and Juliet* is a tragedy based on (　　).
   (a) an English legend　　　　(b) a science-fiction story
   (c) an Italian folk story　　　(d) a true story
3. The phrase *in deep conflict* in line 5 means (　　).
   (a) opposed to each other　　(b) afraid of each other
   (c) uniting with each other　　(d) on good terms with each other
4. The letters addressed to Juliet are sent (　　).
   (a) to request to see the plays of Shakespeare
   (b) to ask to be invited to visit Juliet's grave
   (c) to praise Shakespeare's literature
   (d) to ask Juliet's advice about love
5. Tourists who want good luck in love touch the (　　) of Juliet's statue.
   (a) right arm　　(b) left foot　　(c) right breast　　(d) left shoulder

Exercise 2 次の各文が本文の内容に合っていればT(True)，合っていなければF(False)を書きなさい。

_____ 1. Romantic stories have been passed down since ancient times.
_____ 2. *Romeo and Juliet* is a well-known love story that ends tragically for the two lovers.
_____ 3. Juliet was a real person who lived in Verona hundreds of years ago.
_____ 4. "Juliet's Club" is an office that provides information for tourists who visit Verona.
_____ 5. Tourists who visit Juliet's House don't care that Juliet didn't really exist.

Read Aloud

強く発音するところ（9か所）の○を黒く塗りつぶし，ポーズを置くところ（2か所）に／を書き入れ，CDを聞いて音読しなさい。

Love is one of life's greatest concerns for men and women, young and old.
○　○　○　○　　○　　　　○　　○　○　○　　　○　　　　○　　○　○

ℹ Information for the Topic

恋の悩みにお答えします！

　ジュリエット・クラブは，様々な経験を持つ「秘書」たちによって運営されています。彼らは多種多様な職業に就き，既婚者，離婚経験者，独身者など，背景も年齢も異なる男女です。日本語で手紙を書いても翻訳して内容に目を通し，返事を返してくれます。もし恋の悩みがあるなら，ジュリエット・クラブに相談してはどうでしょうか。

Unit 4

Grammar Section
現在形・過去形

Grammar Points

▶ 動詞が表す動作や状態がいつ起こったかという時間的概念は動詞の語形によって表します。

現在形	現在の性質・状態	I **am** 19 years old.
	現在の習慣・反復的動作	I usually **get** up at six.
	普遍的真理・ことわざ	The earth **goes** around the sun.
	確定的な未来	Tomorrow **is** December 24.
過去形	過去の動作・出来事	I **saw** a strange man yesterday.
	過去の習慣・反復的動作	I often **went** shopping with my mother.

▶ 主節に過去形の動詞があるとき，従属節内の動詞も時制の一致を受けて過去形になります。
（ただし，普遍的真理や歴史的事実は時制の一致の影響を受けません。）
She *believed* that he **had** an older brother.（彼女は彼に兄がいると信じていた）

Exercise 1 （　）内に入る最も適切な語句を選びなさい。

1. Everyone who meets Tom (fall / falls / fell) in love with him at a first sight.
2. She (complains / complained) about her ex-boyfriend every time we met.
3. We (celebrate / celebrated / are celebrating) our fifth wedding anniversary yesterday.
4. Cathy (go / goes / went) for a drive along the coast with James almost every weekend even now.

Exercise 2 日本語に合うように（　）内に適切な語を書き入れなさい。

1. Our priest told us that a medallion of Maria (　　　　) holders good luck.
（マリアのメダルはそれを持っている人に幸運をもたらすと私たちの神父は言った）
2. On our first date, I (　　　　) my new girlfriend to the cinema.
（最初のデートで，私は新しい恋人を映画に連れて行った）
3. Some people who (　　　　) love troubles (　　　　) fortunetellers for advice.（恋の問題を抱える人の中には，占い師に助言を求める人もいる）
4. It was Shakespeare who first (　　　　), "Love is blind."
（「恋は盲目である」と初めて言ったのはシェイクスピアであった）

Exercise 3 （　）内の語を並べかえて英文を完成させなさい。

1. Mary and Jim's romance (to / ending / month / unhappy / last / came / an).

2. I am (warm / to / people / the / attracted / have / heart / who).

3. I (a / years / hear / Emi / ago / that / divorce / got / five).

Unit 5 Transportation

Listening Section

> **Listening Tips**
>
> 消える音Ⅱ ―**what time** はどう聞こえる?―
>
> [p][t][k][b][d][g] の音が1つ目の単語の語末と2つ目の単語の語頭に連続して現れるとき，1つ目の単語の語末の子音が聞こえにくくなることがあります。例えば，what time では，what の [t] の音が聞こえにくくなり，「ワッタイム」のように聞こえることがあります。
>
> 1. get together   2. hard disk   3. stop point
> 4. whipped cream   5. kept calling   6. white dog

Exercise 1 *Listen to the CD and choose the statement that best describes the picture.*

1. (a)   (b)   (c)   (d)   2. (a)   (b)   (c)   (d)

Exercise 2 *Listen to the CD and choose the best response.*

1. (a)   (b)   (c)   2. (a)   (b)   (c)
3. (a)   (b)   (c)   4. (a)   (b)   (c)

Exercise 3 *Listen to the CD and answer the questions.*

1. Where is the conversation taking place?
    (a) At an airport
    (b) At a ticket counter
    (c) At a travel agency
    (d) In an airplane

2. Why does the man need to pay for his meal?
    (a) His ticket doesn't include the meal charge.
    (b) All passengers must pay the meal charge on board.
    (c) He wants to order an extra meal in addition to the regular one.
    (d) The travel agency made a mistake.

●25

Unit 5

Reading Section
Low-Cost Carriers

Words & Phrases -- 次の語句の意味を選びなさい。

1. transportation ( ) 2. promising ( ) 3. entry ( ) 4. reduce ( )
5. simplify ( ) 6. additional ( ) 7. unify ( )
8. eliminate ( ) 9. prevalent ( ) 10. stimulate ( )

(a) 排除する　(b) 活性化する　(c) 乗り物　(d) 参入　(e) 普及している
(f) 簡略化する　(g) 統一する　(h) 縮小する　(i) 期待のできる　(j) 追加の

次の文を読んで，後の設問に答えなさい。

Reading Passage

　The fastest way to travel is by plane. If time is a major issue, flying is your best bet. When your destination is far away, airplanes are often more comfortable and convenient than any other mode of transportation. Air travel's only weak point is the price of tickets.

　One promising step toward solving the price problem is the entry of low-cost carriers into the aviation industry. Their ticket prices are considerably reduced. How do they manage to stay in business with such low fares? How do they make up for the loss of profit from tickets? They do so mainly by reducing operating costs, cutting labor costs, simplifying in-flight service, and controlling ticket-selling costs.

　Some features of low-cost carriers are:

・Charging additional fees for food, drinks, check-in baggage, etc.
・Dropping in-flight entertainment such as music and video.
・Using secondary airports to take advantage of lower landing fees.
・Having employees perform multiple roles such as having flight attendants clean the aircraft or work as gate agents.
・Unifying the economy class seats and not offering reserved seating.
・Conducting direct ticket sales over the Internet, eliminating commissions.

　Low-cost airlines are becoming more prevalent all over the world. Low-cost carriers allow the budget-conscious traveler to get to his or her destination without "breaking the bank." Low-cost carriers also help increase the number of foreign visitors to any country, stimulating tourism and the entire economy.

(230 words)

bet 手段　　aviation industry 航空業界　　make up for ~ ~を補う　　in-flight 機内の
secondary airport 第2の空港（基幹空港を補完するために都心から遠く離れたところに設けられた，着陸料が安い空港）
landing fee 着陸料　　gate agent 空港のゲート係員　　commission 委託手数料
budget-conscious 経費が気になる　　break the bank 破産する

Transportation

Exercise 1 （　）内に入る最も適切な語句を選び，文を完成させなさい。

1. This passage's main focus is on (　) of low-cost carriers.
   (a) the history　(b) the features　(c) the prices　(d) the problems
2. Airplanes are most comfortable and convenient when the place that you're (　) is far away.
   (a) going to　(b) staying at　(c) starting from　(d) returning to
3. Low-cost carriers (　) additional fees for food, drinks, and check-in baggage.
   (a) pay　(b) refuse　(c) neglect　(d) charge
4. Flight attendants perform (　) roles such as cleaning the aircraft or working as gate agents.
   (a) various　(b) professional　(c) important　(d) unimportant
5. The word *stimulating* in line 21 means (　).
   (a) delivering　(b) detecting　(c) developing　(d) designing

Exercise 2 次の各文が本文の内容に合っていればT(True)，合っていなければF(False)を書きなさい。

_____ 1. No other means of transportation is better than flying when time is the main concern.
_____ 2. Air travel is the cheapest of all means of transportation.
_____ 3. Low-cost carriers sometimes cut operating costs to make up for the loss of profit from tickets.
_____ 4. All passengers on a low-cost flight can enjoy listening to music and playing video games at no charge.
_____ 5. Low-cost air travel is suitable for passengers who don't mind fewer comforts or limited services.

Read Aloud 強く発音するところ（8か所）の○を黒く塗りつぶし，ポーズを置くところ（1か所）に／を書き入れ，CDを聞いて音読しなさい。 *T-CD 1-36*

Airplanes are often more comfortable than any other mode of transportation.
○　　○　○　　　○　　○　　　　　　○ ○ ○　　○ ○　　　　　○

ℹ Information for the Topic

LCC（格安航空会社）と安全性

　公共の交通機関は何よりも安全第一で，「安かろう，危なかろう」では困ります。格安だからといって安全面を犠牲にして整備費用を削っているわけではありません。当局（日本の場合「国交省」）の基準をクリアして事業認可・免許を受けて運航していますので，安全基準に関しては大手航空会社と同じで，LCCだから危険ということは基本的には考えられません。ちなみに，LCCの代表格，Southwest Airlines（アメリカ 1967年），Ryanair（アイルランド 1985年），Easy Jet（イギリス 1995年）は創業以来，乗客・乗員の死亡事故はゼロです。

Unit 5

Grammar Section
未来を表す表現

Grammar Points

▶ 未来に起こる予定の出来事を表現するときは will や be going to を用います。

will	主語＋will＋動詞の原形	Sue **will** be 20 next birthday.
be going to	主語＋be going to＋動詞の原形	Sue **is going to** be a nurse.

✎ will はその場で決められた未来の意志や客観的判断を，be going to は前もって決められた未来の計画や主観的判断を表します。

▶「今まさに～するところだ」という近接した未来を表すには be about to を用います。
　The cherry blossoms **are about to** bloom.（桜の花が今まさに開花しようとしている）

▶ 往来発着を表す動詞では現在形や現在進行形で確定的な未来の予定を表します。
　We **start** for London tomorrow morning.（私たちは明日の朝ロンドンに出発します）

▶ 時や条件を表す副詞節の中では，未来の出来事も現在形で表します。
　Please lock the door when you **leave**.（出かける時はドアに鍵をかけてください）

Exercise 1 （　）内に入る最も適切な語句を選びなさい。

1. Hurry up, or you (will miss / missed) the last train.

2. We (are going to / are about to) enter the expressway in ten minutes.

3. I'll call you after I (arrive / will arrive) at the airport.

4. I (will take / was going to take) the flight tomorrow, but it has been canceled.

Exercise 2 日本語に合うように（　）内に適切な語を書き入れなさい。

1. We (　　　　) be late. I know a short cut to the airport.
　（遅れそうです。私は空港への近道を知ってます）

2. The public transportation system is (　　　　) to enter the age of the linear motor car.（公共交通機関は今まさにリニアモーターカーの時代に突入しようとしている）

3. We are (　　　　) to take a taxi to the station.（駅までタクシーに乗るつもりです）

4. The next bus (　　　　) at 3:45.（次のバスは3時45分に来ます）

Exercise 3 （　）内の語を並べかえて英文を完成させなさい。

1. How long (the / be / will / delayed / flight)?

2. When we arrived at the platform, (to / about / train / was / just / leave / the).

3. I'll take a ship (go / time / if / Hokkaido / next / to / I).

Unit 6　Business

Listening Section

Listening Tips

消える音Ⅲ　―**good job** はどう聞こえる？―

語末の [p][t][k][b][d][g] と語頭の [tʃ][dʒ], [f][v][s][h][ʃ], [m][n] が連続する場合，1つ目の単語の語末の子音は聞こえにくくなることがあります。例えば，good job では，good の [d] の音が聞こえにくくなり，「グッジョブ」のように聞こえることがあります。

1. pop music　　　　2. great chance　　　3. black fish
4. club sandwich　　5. good morning　　　6. big chance

Exercise 1　Listen to the CD and choose the statement that best describes the picture.

1. (a)　(b)　(c)　(d)　　　　2. (a)　(b)　(c)　(d)

Exercise 2　Listen to the CD and choose the best response.

1. (a)　(b)　(c)　　　　　2. (a)　(b)　(c)
3. (a)　(b)　(c)　　　　　4. (a)　(b)　(c)

Exercise 3　Listen to the CD and answer the questions.

1. Who is the speaker?
    (a) A health-food store clerk
    (b) A Japanese seasoning retailer
    (c) A restaurant customer
    (d) A restaurant owner

2. What did one customer suggest that the speaker do?
    (a) Add some soy sauce to his dishes
    (b) Serve miso soup with his dishes
    (c) Make some dishes more suitable for children
    (d) Mix in more exotic spices

Unit 6

Reading Section
An Indian Restaurateur

Words & Phrases 次の語句の意味を選びなさい。

1. exotic (　)　2. manage (　)　3. get started (　)
4. establish (　)　5. headquarters (　)　6. strive (　)
7. crucial (　)　8. situated (　)　9. spacious (　)　10. adapt (　)

(a) 大切な　(b) 確立する　(c) 努力する　(d) 経営する　(e) 本部
(f) 位置している　(g) 適合させる　(h) 珍しい　(i) 広々とした　(j) 始める

次の文を読んで，後の設問に答えなさい。

Reading Passage

　If you are hoping for an exotic, spicy, tasty meal, Indian cooking might be just the right choice. Mr. Govinda, aged 30, is an Indian businessman who is climbing the road to success. He and his wife, Radha, manage a popular Indian restaurant in Osaka.

Interviewer: How did you get started in your business?

Mr. Govinda: My wife's father started the Vishnu chain of Indian restaurants more than thirty years ago. Today, the chain has some twenty restaurants mainly based in Kyushu. Last year, after getting married, I decided I would like to go into business for myself. So now, as a first step, I am managing a restaurant owned by my father-in-law.

I: What do you think are the keys to success in the restaurant business?

G: Healthy, delicious, high-quality food coupled with good service will win many customers. The most important thing is to establish a brand image as a fine Indian restaurant. In the Vishnu chain, to do this, we train all our chefs in Indian cooking at our headquarters kitchen. We strive to maintain the high quality of our food at every restaurant in the chain. Of course, location is crucial to success as well. Being situated within five to six minutes' walk from a station is best, and a spacious parking area nearby is a must. These two factors bring in many new customers each day.

I: What do you do to attract Japanese customers?

G: It is important for us to know our Japanese customers well and to provide for their needs. By constantly adapting our dishes to Japanese tastes and eating styles, we hope to increase their support. We offer daily specials, bite-size *tandoori* chicken, take-out *nan* (flat bread), and all kinds of other "attractions" that appeal to Japanese customers.

(297 words)

restaurateur レストラン経営者　father-in-law 義父　coupled with ~ ~と合わせる　a must 不可欠なもの
daily special 日替わり定食　bite-size 一口サイズの　tandoori インドの大かまど(タンドール)で焼いた

Exercise 1 （　　）内に入る最も適切な語句を選び，文を完成させなさい。

1. The main idea of the passage is how to (　　).
   (a) deal with Japanese customers　　(b) cook delicious Indian dishes
   (c) produce skilled Indian chefs　　(d) succeed in the restaurant business
2. An Indian restaurant usually serves exotic, (　　), delicious food.
   (a) hot　　　　(b) mild　　　　(c) bitter　　　　(d) cheap
3. Mr. Govinda suggests that the most important thing to succeed is to establish (　　).
   (a) a training system　　(b) a brand image
   (c) high-quality spices　　(d) a spacious parking area
4. Mr. Govinda is adapting his dishes to Japanese tastes to (　　).
   (a) open a new restaurant　　(b) introduce Indian spices
   (c) get a better location　　(d) increase Japanese support
5. The word *attractions* in line 23 means (　　).
   (a) people who do something interesting　　(b) interesting places to go
   (c) performances and shows　　(d) interesting things to eat

Exercise 2 次の各文が本文の内容に合っていればT(True)，合っていなければF(False)を書きなさい。

_____ 1. Mr. Govinda started his Indian restaurant about thirty years ago.
_____ 2. The Vishnu chain has more than thirty restaurants in the Kyoto area.
_____ 3. All the chefs in the Vishnu chain are trained in the kitchen at the chain's headquarters.
_____ 4. Mr. Govinda says that the best location is right next to a train station.
_____ 5. Mr. Govinda is constantly trying to attract Japanese customers with new ideas.

Read Aloud 強く発音するところ（7か所）の○を黒く塗りつぶし，ポーズを置くところ（3か所）に／を書き入れ，CDを聞いて音読しなさい。

After getting married, I decided I would like to go into business for myself.
○　　　○　　　○　　　○　　　○　　　○　　　○　　　○○　　　○　　　○　　　○

Information for the Topic

ナン (nan)

日本のインド料理店で人気のあるナン（nan）は，インド，西アジア，中央アジアなどの平焼きパンのことで，小麦粉を水でこねて発酵させ，薄くのばして，タンドールと呼ばれる壺型のかまどの内側に貼り付けて焼いたものです。ナンはかまどを持つ上流階級のインド人の家ではよく食べられていますが，一般的なインド人家庭ではあまり食べられていません。インド人の多くは鉄板などで焼くことができるチャパティと呼ばれるパンを食べています。

Unit 6

Grammar Section
進 行 形

Grammar Points

▶限られた期間の間だけ進行する動作や状態を表す時は動詞の進行形を用います。

現在進行形	主語＋is／are＋現在分詞	It **is snowing** now.
過去進行形	主語＋was／were＋現在分詞	It **was snowing** yesterday.
未来進行形	主語＋will be＋現在分詞	It **will be snowing** tomorrow.

▶現在時制は現在の一般的事実や習慣，現在進行形は現時点の一時的な現象や活動を表します。
　　She usually **wears** glasses.（彼女はふだん眼鏡をかけています）＜習慣＞
　　She **is wearing** contacts today.（彼女は今日コンタクトをしています）＜一時的状態＞
▶状態を表す動詞や受動的な知覚を表す動詞は，通常，進行形にしないで用います。
　　She **resembles** her mother.（× She is resembling …）（彼女は母親に似ている）
　　I **know** that he is innocent.（× I'm knowing …）（私は彼が無実なことを知っている）

Exercise 1　(　) 内に入る最も適切な語句を選びなさい。

1. We (will be planning / are planning) to meet with your company this month.
2. When I called on the client, he (talked / was talking) on the phone.
3. At this time next year, Janet (will work / will be working) in Hawaii.
4. He (owns / is owning) five Italian restaurants in Tokyo.

Exercise 2　日本語に合うように (　) 内に適切な語を書き入れなさい。

1. Our company (　　　　) now (　　　　) assistance robots for elderly people.（弊社は今，高齢者向けの介助ロボットを販売しています）
2. What (　　　　) your father (　　　　) for a living?
（あなたのお父さんはどんな仕事をされていますか）
3. Mr. Yamada (　　　　)(　　　　) the sales department at the moment.
（山田さんは現在，営業部に所属しています）
4. I (　　　　)(　　　　) a client today, but he just called to change the date.
（今日，得意先と会う予定だったが，先ほど先方から日程を変更したいと電話があった）

Exercise 3　(　) 内の語を並べかえて英文を完成させなさい。

1. Will you (office / by / coming / the / to / be / bicycle) tomorrow?

2. When she got married, Emi (hotel / for / working / five-star / was / a) in Osaka.

3. He (about / is / income / always / small / complaining / his).

Unit 7 Society

Listening Section

Listening Tips

つながる音Ⅰ　—an orange はどう聞こえる？—

子音で終わる単語の次に母音が続く場合，音がつながって1語のようになめらかに発音されることがあります。例えば，an orange は an の語末の子音 [n] と orange の語頭の母音 [ɔ] がつながり，「アノーレンジ」のように聞こえます。この現象は語末が [n] の場合にはっきりと現れ，速く話されるときだけでなく，普通の速度やゆっくり話されるときでも起こります。

1. in English
2. turn on
3. an orange
4. run away
5. kick off
6. hold on

Exercise 1 Listen to the CD and choose the statement that best describes the picture.

1. (a)　(b)　(c)　(d)
2. (a)　(b)　(c)　(d)

Exercise 2 Listen to the CD and choose the best response.

1. (a)　(b)　(c)
2. (a)　(b)　(c)
3. (a)　(b)　(c)
4. (a)　(b)　(c)

Exercise 3 Listen to the CD and answer the questions.

1. Why did Yuki look especially happy today?
   (a) She became a leader of the Girl Scouts.
   (b) She joined the UNHCR.
   (c) She collected a lot of money for refugees.
   (d) She visited the United Nations.

2. Which of the following statements is true?
   (a) The man knew well about UNHCR.
   (b) The money people donated was less than Yuki had expected.
   (c) Yuki has been a member of the Girl Scouts for a long time.
   (d) Yuki was once a refugee herself.

● 33

Unit 7

Reading Section
Global Self-Help Revolution

Words & Phrases 次の語句の意味を選びなさい。

1. found (　) 2. valid (　) 3. organization (　) 4. rebuild (　)
5. publish (　) 6. budget (　) 7. distribute (　)
8. voluntary (　) 9. donation (　) 10. challenge (　)

(a) 組織　(b) 発行する　(c) 立て直す　(d) 生活費　(e) 任意の
(f) 寄付　(g) 正当な　(h) 設立する　(i) 課題　(j) 流通させる

次の文を読んで，後の設問に答えなさい。

Reading Passage

　The Big Issue was founded in 1991 in the U.K. by Gordon Roddick and John Bird. Its magazine, *The Big Issue*, has been addressing the problem of homelessness by offering homeless people the opportunity to earn a valid income on their own. Many famous people such as Angelina Jolie and Prince William have been interviewed in its
5　pages. Created as a business solution to a social problem, the Big Issue has become a powerful blueprint for social change, and has led to the creation of hundreds of similar organizations around the world.

　The Big Issue Japan was created in 2003 to help homeless people rebuild their lives. It publishes a high-quality magazine, *The Big Issue Japan*, twice a month, which is
10　sold by vendors who are all homeless.

　The system works as follows. First, prospective vendors must prove they are homeless. Then they are given ten free copies of the magazine to sell. Once they have sold the ten copies at 350 yen each, they can buy more copies at 170 yen each. They make 180 yen for each copy they sell. In this way, homeless people can earn money
15　and learn to manage their budgets.

　From September 2003 to September 2013, 1,467 homeless people were registered as vendors. By March 2014, about 6.3 million copies of *The Big Issue Japan* had been distributed, earning vendors some 894 million yen.

　Earning an income is the first step. The Big Issue Japan goes further and
20　offers four important supports toward independence: housing, health, financial independence, and, most importantly, hope. The organization also relies heavily on voluntary donations. The Big Issue can be seen as a challenge to society as well as to vendors.

(282 words)

address 取り組む　Angelina Jolie アンジェリーナ・ジョリー(1975-) アメリカの女優
Prince William ウィリアム王子(1982-) 英国の王子　　blueprint 青写真
prospective vendor 販売者になろうとする人　　copy (雑誌などの)一冊

34

 Society

Exercise 1 （　　）内に入る最も適切な語句を選び，文を完成させなさい。

1. The Big Issue aims first of all to give homeless people the chance to (　　).
   (a) live in a house　　　　　　　　(b) earn an income on their own
   (c) cooperate with each other　　　(d) be healthy
2. To become vendors, candidates must first prove that they have (　　).
   (a) no money　　(b) no family　　(c) no friends　　(d) nowhere to live
3. The word *Once* in line 12 means (　　).
   (a) Why　　　　(b) When　　　　(c) Where　　　　(d) How
4. After selling ten free copies at (　　) yen each, vendors can buy more copies.
   (a) 170　　　　(b) 180　　　　(c) 200　　　　(d) 350
5. The most important support from the organization besides earning money is offering (　　).
   (a) financial independence　　(b) housing　　(c) hope　　(d) entertainment

Exercise 2 次の各文が本文の内容に合っていればT(True)，合っていなければF(False)を書きなさい。

_____ 1. The Big Issue was first established in the U.S. more than 30 years ago.
_____ 2. Many famous people have appeared on the interview pages of *The Big Issue*.
_____ 3. There are nearly 100 organizations similar to the Big Issue around the world.
_____ 4. The vendors can earn 180 yen from each copy of *The Big Issue* that they sell after they have sold the initial 10 copies.
_____ 5. The Big Issue Japan relies only on donations.

Read Aloud　強く発音するところ(7か所)の○を黒く塗りつぶし，ポーズを置くところ(2か所)に／を書き入れ，CDを聞いて音読しなさい。　T-CD 1-50

The Big Issue can be seen as a challenge to society as well as to
○ ○ ○　　　　○ ○ ○ ○ ○ ○ ○　　　　○ ○ ○ ○ ○ ○
vendors.
○

ℹ Information for the Topic

若者のホームレス

　2008年のリーマンショック以来，日本で「若者のホームレス」が増えています。彼らは自立していく段階で様々な不利な条件が障害となって，不安定な単純労務の世界に入ることを余儀なくされています。そこから，ホームレスの状態につながっていく可能性があります。ひきこもり，若年無業者（ニート），フリーターが多く存在する現在，多くの若者がホームレスに近い距離にいるとも考えられます。ホームレスが立ち直るためには，「仕事」，「住居」だけでなく，「人間的つながり」，「自己肯定感」なども必要不可欠です。

Unit 7

Grammar Section
完 了 形

Grammar Points

▶完了形は，時間軸上のある時点を基準にして，その時点までの動作の完了や継続を表します。

現在完了	have／has＋過去分詞	I **have** just **finished** reading a book.（完了）
過去完了	had＋過去分詞	He **had** never **seen** the sea before the age of eleven.（経験）
未来完了	will have＋過去分詞	I **will have been** ill in bed for a week by tomorrow.（継続）

▶現在完了は，現在とつながりのある過去の出来事を表す点で過去時制とは異なります。
　[現在完了] I **have lived** in Nara for ten years.（奈良に10年住んでいる）＜今も住んでいる＞
　[過去時制] I **lived** in Nara for ten years.（奈良に10年住んでいた）＜今住んでいるかは不明＞

Exercise 1　（　）内に入る最も適切な語句を選びなさい。

1. We (have / had / will have) been discussing social problems for about an hour when she arrived.

2. (Hasn't / Haven't) your brother ever thought about more important things than money?

3. If I read the book one more time, I (have / will have / had) read it four times.

4. The magazine (will have been / has been / is) sold on newsstands only recently.

Exercise 2　日本語に合うように（　）内に適切な語を書き入れなさい。

1. By the end of 2010, sales of his novel (　　　)(　　　) him thirty million yen.（2010年末までに，小説の売り上げは彼に3,000万円をもたらせていた）

2. He (　　　)(　　　) rebuilt his life by the end of next year.
　（彼は来年末までに人生を立て直しているでしょう）

3. The organization (　　　)(　　　) a driving force for social change these past four years.（その組織はここ4年間で社会変化の原動力となってきた）

4. I (　　　)(　　　) seen a vendor of *The Big Issue* on this street.
　（私は「ビッグイシュー」の販売者をこの通りで一度も見たことがありません）

Exercise 3　（　）内の語を並べかえて英文を完成させなさい。

1. There (no / been / news / society / has / in / good) lately.

2. By the age of twenty, (already / for / name / a / he / made / had) himself as a writer.

3. The economy (the / better / will / turned / for / by / have) the end of next year.

Unit 8　Health

Listening Section

Listening Tips

つながる音 II　—**far away** はどう聞こえる？—

far away や never again のように，２語の間に強い意味のつながりがある場合，前の単語の語末の [r] と次の単語の語頭の母音がつながって聞こえることがあります．特に [r] は単独では聞こえにくい音ですが，後に続く語頭の母音の影響を受けてはっきりと聞こえるようになります．例えば，far away は「ファーアウェイ」ではなく，「ファラウェイ」と聞こえます．

1. cheer up　　　　　2. after all　　　　　3. far away
4. more important　　5. never again　　　　6. care about

Exercise 1　Listen to the CD and choose the statement that best describes the picture.

1.　(a)　(b)　(c)　(d)　　　2.　(a)　(b)　(c)　(d)

Exercise 2　Listen to the CD and choose the best response.

1.　(a)　(b)　(c)　　　　　2.　(a)　(b)　(c)
3.　(a)　(b)　(c)　　　　　4.　(a)　(b)　(c)

Exercise 3　Listen to the CD and answer the questions.

1. Why did Mr. Adams visit the doctor's office?
    (a) His children had health problems.
    (b) He needed some advice about his job.
    (c) He was having trouble sleeping.
    (d) He wanted to stop drinking.

2. Which of the following statements is true?
    (a) Mr. Adams worked for a drug company.
    (b) Mr. Adams lost his job.
    (c) The doctor told Mr. Adams to take a warm bath before bed.
    (d) Mr. Adams was given some sleeping medicine.

Unit 8

Reading Section
Achilles Tendon Rupture

Words & Phrases --- 次の語句の意味を選びなさい。

1. injury (　)　2. fracture (　)　3. echo (　)　4. naturally (　)
5. surgeon (　)　6. cast (　)　7. crutch (　)　8. bandage (　)
9. secure (　)　10. recover (　)

(a) 外科医　(b) けが　(c) 回復する　(d) 骨折　(e) ギブス
(f) 響く　(g) 安全にする　(h) 松葉杖　(i) もちろん・自然に　(j) 包帯

次の文を読んで，後の設問に答えなさい。

Reading Passage

When we play sports or exercise, serious injury is always a risk. Fracture is, of course, a common, sports-related injury. Another is an Achilles tendon rupture.

I ruptured mine during an aerobics class. Suddenly, a loud popping sound echoed in the room. I had no pain, but I couldn't walk. Naturally, I was taken to the hospital right away.

My surgeon explained that there were two options for an Achilles tendon rupture: nonsurgical and surgical. Nonsurgical therapy waits for the tendon to heal naturally. The injured leg is put in a cast for six to eight weeks. Once the cast is removed, a long period of rehabilitation gets underway. For the first month, we can walk only with the help of crutches.

I chose the surgical option. I thought it would be better because my surgeon told me there was less chance of re-rupture. The surgery took about two hours, after which I spent three days in the hospital. After returning home, I spent about one month walking on crutches, with a bandage to secure the foot above the ground. When I no longer needed the crutches, I had to wear a boot for another month both inside and outside the house. This was because my foot had to be kept fixed at a certain angle. That's when the long rehabilitation started. Now, one year since my injury, I still have not fully recovered.

Sometimes I ask myself why this happened to me. Was it beyond my control? One thing I can absolutely say, though, is that we need to warm up before we exercise and to cool down after. Repentance comes too late!

(274 words)

Achilles tendon rupture アキレス腱断裂　aerobics エアロビクス　popping sound バチッという音
surgical 手術による　get underway 行われる　boot（治療用）長靴
Repentance comes too late.（ことわざ）後悔先に立たず

Health

Exercise 1 （　）内に入る最も適切な語句を選び，文を完成させなさい。

1. The author's Achilles tendon rupture was caused while (　　).
   (a) wearing high heels　(b) running　(c) exercising　(d) playing golf
2. The author was taken to the hospital (　　) after being injured.
   (a) a few hours　(b) immediately　(c) six to eight hours　(d) a few days
3. The word *heal* in line 7 means (　　).
   (a) to put an end　　　　　　　(b) to give medical treatment
   (c) to become healthy again　(d) to calm down
4. The author's doctor suggested nonsurgical therapy had (　　) chance of re-rupture.
   (a) less　(b) more　(c) the least　(d) the most
5. The author firmly believes that we should do some (　　) before playing a sport.
   (a) warm-up exercise　　　(b) easy exercise
   (c) cool-down exercise　　(d) hard exercise

Exercise 2 次の各文が本文の内容に合っていればT(True)，合っていなければF(False)を書きなさい。

_____ 1. The author felt a severe pain when she ruptured her Achilles tendon.
_____ 2. A ruptured Achilles tendon heals naturally with proper treatment.
_____ 3. After the surgery, the author went home without having to stay in the hospital.
_____ 4. When the author no longer needed crutches, she walked around freely indoors.
_____ 5. The author was fully recovered from her injury after a few months' rehabilitation.

Read Aloud 強く発音するところ（7か所）の○を黒く塗りつぶし，ポーズを置くところ（1か所）に／を書き入れ，CDを聞いて音読しなさい。

The injured leg is put in a cast for six to eight weeks.

Information for the Topic

悪夢再び!?

　アキレス腱断裂をした患者が最も恐れるのは，同じ場所を再度断裂することと，もう一方の足のアキレスを断裂すること（逆足断裂）です。それらを心配することは患者にとって相当大きな心理的負担になります。中には4回，5回の再断裂の記録もあります。他に，両足アキレス腱断裂というのをまれに耳にしますが，アキレス腱断裂の中ではもっとも悲惨な断裂です。歩行は不可能となり，長期間の車いす生活を強いられ，日常生活に大きな支障をきたします。

Unit 8

Grammar Section
助 動 詞

Grammar Points

▶助動詞は本動詞の意味を補い，可能・推量・許可・義務などの意味を付け加えます。

can	能力・可能（～できる）	Everybody in this class **can** swim.
	[否定文で] 否定推量（～はずがない）	That woman **cannot** be very old.
may	許可（～してよい）	**May** I come in?
	推量（～かもしれない）	You **may** miss the last train.
must	義務・強要（～しなければならない）	You **must** keep your room clean.
	推量（～にちがいない）	The English teacher **must** be ill.
	[否定文で] 禁止（～してはいけない）	You **must** not smoke here.
should ought to	義務・当然（～すべきだ）	You **should** go to the dentist soon. We **ought to** save energy.
would	過去の習慣（よく～したものだ）	I **would** often go fishing with him.

Exercise 1 （　）内に入る最も適切な語句を選びなさい。

1. I (mustn't / can't) believe that he died of lung cancer after such a short time.

2. Before an operation, doctors (should / may) get consent from the family.

3. When you take this medicine, you (will / should) often feel sleepy and thirsty.

4. I asked the doctor how I (would / should) take the medicine.

Exercise 2　日本語に合うように（　）内に適切な語を書き入れなさい。

1. The patient (　　　　　) be over fifty.（その患者は 50 歳を超えているにちがいない）

2. It (　　　　　) take a year to recover from the illness.
   （病気からの回復に 1 年はかかるかもしれません）

3. You (　　　　　) not to touch your left foot on the ground.
   （左足を地面につけてはいけません）

4. That young nurse (　　　　　) often bring me an ice bag.
   （その若い看護師が私によく氷枕をもってきてくれた）

Exercise 3 （　）内の語を並べかえて英文を完成させなさい。

1. The nurse said, "(are / old / ask / I / you / how / may / you)?"

   _____

2. You (tomorrow / eat / regular / can / meals / starting).

   _____

3. I'd (with / an / like / make / to / appointment / Dr. Smith).

   _____

Unit 9 The Environment

Listening Section

Listening Tips

つながる音Ⅲ　―**Come on in.** はどう聞こえる？―

　Come on in. のように３語以上であっても，各語の間に強い意味のつながりがある場合，それぞれの単語の語末の子音と続く単語の語頭の母音は音がつながることがあります。これにより Come on in. は「カモニン」と１語のようになめらかに聞こえます。音がつながることにより，どこからどこまでが１つの単語なのかがわかりにくくなります。

1. Come on in.
2. kick it off
3. fill it up
4. run out of oil
5. turn off an engine
6. live in an apartment

Exercise 1　Listen to the CD and choose the statement that best describes the picture.

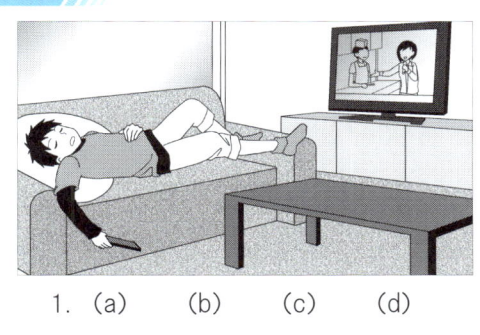

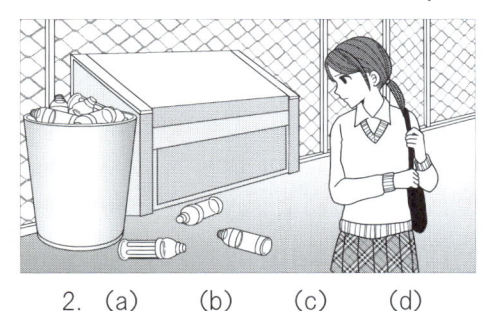

1. (a)　(b)　(c)　(d)　　2. (a)　(b)　(c)　(d)

Exercise 2　Listen to the CD and choose the best response.

1. (a)　(b)　(c)　　　　2. (a)　(b)　(c)
3. (a)　(b)　(c)　　　　4. (a)　(b)　(c)

Exercise 3　Listen to the CD and answer the questions.

1. What does Susan do to practice the 3R?
    (a) She reads the newspaper every day.
    (b) She recycles aluminum cans.
    (c) She carries disposable wooden chopsticks everywhere.
    (d) She tries not to use convenience stores.

2. Which of the following statements is true?
    (a) There is little Susan can do for the future of the planet.
    (b) No one used aluminum cans at the party last week.
    (c) Susan does what she can to be environment-friendly.
    (d) Susan's friend thinks she could do much more to save our planet.

Unit 9

Reading Section
Aluminum-can Recycling

Words & Phrases -- 次の語句の意味を選びなさい。

1. cooperative (　)   2. consumer (　)   3. promote (　)   4. benefit (　)
5. save (　)   6. raw materials (　)   7. requirements (　)
8. toss (　)   9. household (　)   10. garbage bag (　)

(a) ためになる   (b) 節約する   (c) 協力的な   (d) 消費者   (e) 捨てる
(f) 促進させる   (g) 必要なもの (h) 家庭   (i) 原材料   (j) ゴミ袋

次の文を読んで，後の設問に答えなさい。

Reading Passage

　Few people know that Brazil is the world champion of aluminum-can recycling. Its recycling rate is an amazingly high 98.3%. Brazil's success is due to the cooperative efforts of aluminum-sheet manufacturers, can manufacturers, recycling companies, consumers, the government, and many others. Recycling is promoted through state-sponsored recycling education programs. Brazil even has a National Aluminum Recycling Day.

　Aluminum-can recycling can benefit the environment in many ways. For one, it saves energy and prevents environmental damage. New aluminum cans are made from raw materials, mainly bauxite (an ore not found in Japan). This process requires huge amounts of energy. But starting the production process from recycled cans cuts energy requirements by about 97%. So you can see how energy efficient it is to recycle aluminum cans. Japan's recycling rate has been some 90% for the last ten years. The average cost of recycling a 500-milliliter can is as low as 0.21 yen.

　Another way recycling helps the environment is that there is no limit to how many times aluminum cans can be recycled. Additionally, in the recycling process, there is no loss of aluminum. Every can tossed into a recycling bin is completely recycled.

　You should know that if we can achieve 100% recycling of aluminum (including aluminum products other than cans), Japan can save about 13 days' worth of household electricity every year. This is equivalent to a savings of 142 billion yen in household electric bills. So the next time you're about to toss an aluminum can into a plastic garbage bag, stop and toss it into the nearest recycling bin instead.

(263 words)

aluminum-sheet manufacturer アルミニウムの薄板製造業者　　state-sponsored 国が支援する　　ore 鉱石
bin ゴミ入れ　　electric bills 電気料金の請求書

The Environment

Exercise 1 （　）内に入る最も適切な語句を選び，文を完成させなさい。

1. Aluminum-can recycling saves energy and can prevent (　　).
   (a) damage to raw materials　　(b) natural disasters
   (c) damage to the environment　　(d) harm to the economy
2. The Brazilian government sponsors (　　) for recycling.
   (a) TV programs　(b) education programs　(c) TV advertisements　(d) consumer events
3. The word *bauxite* in line 9 means the ore from which aluminum is (　　).
   (a) produced　　(b) recycled　　(c) broken down　　(d) saved
4. Starting the manufacturing process for aluminum cans from recycled cans requires only (　) percent of the energy needed to start it from raw materials.
   (a) 3　　(b) 13　　(c) 30　　(d) 97
5. If you toss an aluminum can into a recycling bin, it'll be recycled (　　).
   (a) with only a small amount of waste　　(b) without any waste
   (c) with a lot of waste　　(d) with only 10 percent waste

Exercise 2 次の各文が本文の内容に合っていればT(True)，合っていなければF(False)を書きなさい。

_____ 1. Most people know that Brazil has the world's highest rate of aluminum-can recycling.
_____ 2. Brazil's success in aluminum recycling is mainly due to the efforts of consumers.
_____ 3. Japan's recycling rate of aluminum cans was 10 percent lower ten years ago.
_____ 4. Only 0.21 yen is needed to recycle a 500-milliliter aluminum can.
_____ 5. If Japan can achieve a 100 percent recycling rate in aluminum, we can save about two weeks' worth of household electricity every year.

Read Aloud 強く発音するところ（8か所）の○を黒く塗りつぶし，ポーズを置くところ（3か所）に／を書き入れ，CDを聞いて音読しなさい。

So you can see how energy efficient it is to recycle aluminum cans.
○　○　○　○　○　○　　○　　○○○　○　　○　　　○

Information for the Topic

プラスチックのリサイクル

　プラスチックは大変身近で，われわれの生活に利便性や安全性を与えてくれます。しかし，その組成のほとんどは石油であり，微生物がプラスチックを分解するには1,000万年を要すると言われています。そのため，使用済みプラスチックをリサイクルしたり，各自治体が推奨する適切な分別方法に従って廃棄することが，環境保護にとって大変重要です。昨今，ペットボトル，発泡スチロール，食品トレイなどのリサイクルは普及してきていますが，今後さらにプラスチック製品のリサイクル率を高め，限りある石油資源を有効に使用することが求められています。

Unit 9

Grammar Section

受 動 態

Grammar Points

▶ 動作を行う側が主語になる能動態に対し，受動態は動作を受ける側が主語になり，「～される」という意味を表します。

能動態	主語＋動詞＋目的語（＋目的語／補語）	Many people **loved** the movie.
受動態	主語＋be 動詞＋過去分詞（＋by ～）	The movie **was loved** by many people.

[助動詞を含む場合] Your homework **must be finished** by tomorrow.
[群動詞を含む場合] The player **was looked up to** by all the members of the team.
[by 以外の前置詞を用いる場合] The top of the mountain **is covered with** snow.
　　　　　　　　　　　　　　I **was surprised at** the news.
[2通りの受動態が可能な場合] **It is said that** the plan was very successful.
　　　　　　　　　　　　　　= The plan **is said to** have been very successful.

Exercise 1 （　）内に入る最も適切な語句を選びなさい。

1. A new recycling center is (building / being built) in the city.
2. Environmentalists were disappointed (for / with) the level of air pollution in the region.
3. It (is said / is saying) that the amount of carbon dioxide in the atmosphere is increasing.
4. Can economic growth (be / is) maintained without damaging the environment?

Exercise 2 日本語に合うように（　）内に適切な語を書き入れなさい。

1. I think that all the energy we use should (　　　　) obtained from clean, renewable resources.
（我々が使用するあらゆるエネルギーは，クリーンで再生可能な資源から得られるべきだ）
2. More effort is (　　　　) to end the steady rise in the global population.
（世界人口の絶え間ない増加を終わらせるためにさらなる努力が必要である）
3. The bank has (　　　　) awarded an ISO 14001 for its environmental management system.（その銀行は ISO14001 環境マネジメントシステム規格の認証を得ている）
4. All the restaurant's organic waste is composted and (　　　　) to fertilize the soil.（そのレストランのすべての有機廃棄物は堆肥にされ，土壌を肥沃にするために使われる）

Exercise 3 （　）内の語を並べかえて英文を完成させなさい。

1. Many scientists (global / are / about / in / worried / the / warming / increase).
　
2. Many (environment-friendly / been / have / buildings / constructed) in this town.
　
3. Areas with many different species of animals and types of plants (said / to / are / have / level / high / of / biodiversity / a).

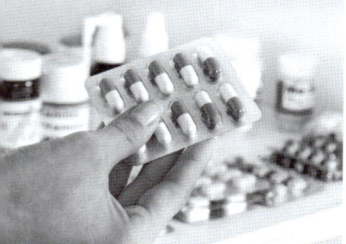

Unit 10 Medicine

Listening Section

Listening Tips

音の同化 I ―**get you** はどう聞こえる?―

語末の [t][d][s][z] などの子音と語頭の [j] の音が連続する場合，その2つの音が影響し合って音声変化が起こることがあります。例えば，get you が「ゲッチュー」, did you が「ディッジュー」のように聞こえることがあります。

1. could you
2. would you
3. miss you
4. as you know
5. this year
6. meet you

Exercise 1 Listen to the CD and choose the statement that best describes the picture.

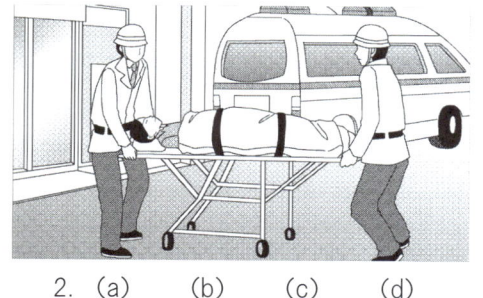

1. (a)　(b)　(c)　(d)　　2. (a)　(b)　(c)　(d)

Exercise 2 Listen to the CD and choose the best response.

1. (a)　(b)　(c)　　　　2. (a)　(b)　(c)
3. (a)　(b)　(c)　　　　4. (a)　(b)　(c)

Exercise 3 Listen to the CD and answer the questions.

1. What is the main topic of the news report?
   (a) Most western doctors like to use acupuncture these days.
   (b) WHO has approved acupuncture as a medical treatment.
   (c) WHO believes that all alternative medicines are effective.
   (d) Every condition or illness can be healed by acupuncture.

2. To Western doctors, what is the downside of alternative medicines?
   (a) They are too expensive.
   (b) There are few doctors who know how to use them.
   (c) Most patients don't trust them.
   (d) There has been no concrete proof of their effectiveness.

Unit 10

Reading Section
Alternative Medicine

Words & Phrases 次の語句の意味を選びなさい。

1. alternative medicine (　)　2. originate (　)　3. harsh (　)
4. acupuncture (　) 5. herbal (　) 6. back pain (　) 7. infection (　)
8. side effect (　)　9. allergic reaction (　)　10. practitioner (　)

(a) 施術者　(b) 副作用　(c) 感染症　(d) 代替医療　(e) 背中の痛み
(f) 起源を持つ　(g) アレルギー反応　(h) 厳しい　(i) ハーブの　(j) 鍼

次の文を読んで，後の設問に答えなさい。

Reading Passage

　Alternative medicine has become popular these days. Some people try alternative medical treatments because they haven't been able to get positive results from Western medicine. How do alternative medicine and Western medicine differ? The biggest difference is that alternative medicine has a milder effect on the body. At the same time, it is risky when it is not used correctly.

　One type of alternative medicine originated in Asia more than 2,000 years ago. People used alternative treatments to prevent illnesses caused by harsh environments. Among these treatments, the best known are acupuncture, massage, and herbal medicine.

　Of these, acupuncture is the most scientifically proven. It is effective to ease back pain, neck pain, and headaches. On the other hand, it may cause nerve damage and infections if the needles are placed incorrectly or not cleaned properly.

　Massage is a simple and convenient treatment method that everyone can benefit from. It can relieve muscle tension and pain without major side effects. Once you learn proper massage techniques, you can even practice them on yourself.

　Herbal treatments can be more dangerous than the others. People tend to think that all herbs are safe since herbs are natural. But poisoning and allergic reactions can occur if they are not used properly. Although herbal medicine is an effective treatment for many conditions, it should only be taken under the guidance of a fully trained practitioner.

　Alternative medicine can be a good complement to Western medicine. But it is not magic or a panacea. You should never depend only on alternative medicine. Always seek a doctor's advice, especially if your illness is serious.

(268 words)

Western medicine 西洋医学　　complement 補完物　　panacea 万能薬

Medicine

Exercise 1 （　）内に入る最も適切な語句を選び，文を完成させなさい。

1. This passage covers the (　　) and risks of alternative medicine.
   (a) difficulties　　(b) benefits　　(c) faults　　(d) challenges
2. The word *prevent* in line 7 means (　　).
   (a) to take care of　　(b) to take into consideration
   (c) to go through　　(d) to stop
3. The effectiveness of acupuncture has been proven based on (　　) evidence.
   (a) traditional　　(b) scientific　　(c) limited　　(d) mistaken
4. Many people think all herbs are safe because they're not (　　).
   (a) exclusive　　(b) domestic　　(c) artificial　　(d) expensive
5. You need to consult a(n) (　　) practitioner if you want to get positive results from herbal medicine.
   (a) inexperienced　　(b) Chinese　　(c) skilled　　(d) gentle

Exercise 2 次の各文が本文の内容に合っていればT(True)，合っていなければF(False)を書きなさい。

_____ 1. The article says that some people try alternative medicine because of the high cost of Western medicine.
_____ 2. People in ancient Asia started to practice alternative medicine to keep from getting sick in harsh environments.
_____ 3. Massage is the most scientifically proven alternative medicine technique.
_____ 4. If herbs are used wrong, poisoning and allergic reactions are possible.
_____ 5. Most serious illnesses can be cured by alternative medicine, so we no longer need Western medicine.

Read Aloud　強く発音するところ（9か所）の○を黒く塗りつぶし，ポーズを置くところ（2か所）に／を書き入れ，CDを聞いて音読しなさい。　T-CD 1-71

One type of alternative medicine originated in Asia a long time ago.
○　　○　　○　　○　　　　　○　　　　○　　　　○○　　○○　　○　　○

Information for the Topic

統合医療

　統合医療とは，西洋医学と東洋医学の両者の長所を取り入れ，国民（患者）中心の全人的医療を目指す医療です。厚生労働省は，東洋医学を西洋医学と統合させようと統合医療プロジェクトチームを発足させました。このプロジェクトチームでは，東洋医学の定義や有用性，利益や不利益，取り組むべき課題や展望が議論されており，これまでの西洋医学と東洋医学の対立ではなく，医療の範囲を広げ，治療だけでなく保健，予防を含む多様な医療を提供しようとしています。

Unit 10

Grammar Section
不定詞

Grammar Points

▶ 不定詞は「to＋動詞の原形」で表され，文中での機能によって3つの用法があります。

名詞的用法	文の主語，目的語，補語になる	He wants **to go** to England.
形容詞的用法	名詞・代名詞を後ろから修飾する	I need something **to drink**.
副詞的用法	動詞や形容詞・副詞を修飾する	They go downtown **to buy** food.

✍ 目的語に不定詞を取る主な動詞：hope, decide, expect, manage, pretend, promise, refuse, wish

✍ 不定詞を含む慣用表現：in order to, so as to, too ... to, enough to, only to, never to

▶ 独立不定詞は文全体を修飾する副詞句の役割を果たします。
　To tell the truth, I don't like her. (実を言うと，私は彼女が好きではありません)

▶ 助動詞の後ろや知覚動詞・使役動詞の目的語の後ろには原形不定詞が使われます。
　We heard the dog **bark** loudly. (私たちは犬が大声で吠えるのを聞いた)

Exercise 1　（　）内に入る最も適切な語句を選びなさい。

1. We hope (to advance / advancing) health-care technology.

2. The newly arrived young doctor seems (being / to be) kind to senior citizens.

3. An increasing number of people live (being / to be) ninety these days.

4. You shouldn't have let the patient (leave / to leave) alone.

Exercise 2　日本語に合うように（　）内に適切な語を書き入れなさい。

1. The doctor was (　　　) busy (　　　) check his own health.
   （その医者は忙しすぎて自分自身の健康状態を調べることができなかった）

2. After a doctor explains various medical treatments, patients decide (　　　) (　　　) choose. (医者が様々な医療行為を示した後，患者がどれを選ぶかを決める)

3. We are delighted (　　　)(　　　) that he is getting better day by day. (彼が日に日に良くなっていることを聞いて，私たちは喜んでいる)

4. I have no (　　　)(　　　) go to get a medical check-up.
   （健康診断に行く時間が私にはありません）

Exercise 3　（　）内の語を並べかえて英文を完成させなさい。

1. It is important (how / stay / shape / to / in / to / know).

2. The key to (less / to / fit / staying / is / eat) and to exercise more.

3. You should get more rest (of / in / reduce / order / your / to / chances) getting sick.

Unit 11　Finance

Listening Section

Listening Tips

音の同化 II　— **nice shot** はどう聞こえる？—

語末の [s] と語頭の [ʃ] が連続すると，後続の音が先行の音に影響を与えて音声変化を起こし，[ʃ] に聞こえることがあります。例えば，nice shot の場合，nice の [s] が shot の [ʃ] の影響を受けて，「ナイショット」のように聞こえることがあります。

1. nice shoes　　　2. space shuttle　　　3. tortoise shell
4. this shop　　　5. less sharp　　　6. famous chef

Exercise 1 Listen to the CD and choose the statement that best describes the picture.

1. (a)　(b)　(c)　(d)　　　2. (a)　(b)　(c)　(d)

Exercise 2 Listen to the CD and choose the best response.

1. (a)　(b)　(c)　　　　2. (a)　(b)　(c)
3. (a)　(b)　(c)　　　　4. (a)　(b)　(c)

Exercise 3 Listen to the CD and answer the questions.

1. Where is this conversation probably taking place?
   (a) At a passport agency
   (b) At a sports club
   (c) In a university laboratory
   (d) In a bank

2. What does the man need to open an account?
   (a) A credit card and insurance
   (b) A driver's license and a passport
   (c) A passport and the signature of a guarantor
   (d) A large deposit and a photograph

● 49

Unit 11

Reading Section
Two Big Players

Words & Phrases 次の語句の意味を選びなさい。

1. millionaire (　)　2. asset (　)　3. active (　)
4. investment (　)　5. stock (　)　6. billion (　)
7. trader (　)　8. firm (　)　9. criticize (　)　10. analyze (　)

(a) 証券業者　(b) 億万長者　(c) 株　(d) 活発な　(e) 10億
(f) 企業　(g) 分析する　(h) 批判する　(i) 投資　(j) 資産

次の文を読んで，後の設問に答えなさい。

Reading Passage

　Have you ever thought about how you can become a millionaire? Work hard and save money? Good advice, but it's not enough. What you need to do is to learn how to increase your assets like Warren Buffett and George Soros, the two most successful "players" in finance.

5　Born in 1930 in Omaha, Nebraska, Buffett was already active in business at age 11. By 13, he had set up his own company. After studying business at three universities, he entered the world of finance. His investment style is sometimes referred to as an "agricultural style." This means finding good firms to invest in and keeping the stocks for a long time — like planting and harvesting a good crop.
10　In 2014, his net worth was estimated at $63 billion.

　The other giant is George Soros, who was born in 1930, in Budapest, Hungary. After surviving the Nazi occupation of Hungary, he moved to the U.K. and graduated from the London School of Economics in 1952. Soros then moved to New York in 1956 and started to work as a financial analyst and trader. Setting up his own
15　investment firm in 1973, he achieved great success through various financial activities. His financial strategies are referred to as a "hunting style." This involves chasing a prey aggressively, for which Soros is sometimes criticized. As of 2014, Soros' net worth was around $23 billion.

　What should you do to become billionaires like Buffett and Soros? First, you
20　need to know finance. Second, you have to be able to analyze market trends. Third, at times, you have to take risks. But for the time being, the key is to work hard and earn the seed money or capital you need to plant and harvest your "crop." (291 words)

player (政治や経済活動などで)影響力の大きい人　　Warren Buffett ウォーレン・バフェット(1930-)アメリカの投資家　　George Soros ジョージ・ソロス(1930-)ハンガリー生まれのアメリカ人投機家　　net worth 純資産　　set up ~ ~を設立する　　prey 獲物　　Nazi occupation ナチスによる占領　　for the time being 当面の間　　capital 資本金

Finance

Exercise 1 （　　）内に入る最も適切な語句を選び，文を完成させなさい。

1. This passage focuses mainly on the two well-known (　　).
   (a) athletes　　(b) politicians　　(c) bankers　　(d) investors
2. To become a millionaire you have to learn how to (　　).
   (a) find a good business partner　　(b) set up a joint venture
   (c) increase your assets　　(d) transfer business overseas
3. Soros set up his own investment firm in (　　).
   (a) 1930　　(b) 1956　　(c) 1973　　(d) 1952
4. The word *aggressively* in line 17 means (　　).
   (a) offensively　　(b) secretly　　(c) gently　　(d) gradually
5. As of 2014, Buffett's net worth is (　　) that of Soros'.
   (a) about half　　(b) about three times
   (c) about twice　　(d) less than

Exercise 2 次の各文が本文の内容に合っていればT(True)，合っていなければF(False)を書きなさい。

_____ 1. Buffett and Soros set up their own companies in their twenties.
_____ 2. Buffett is well-known for his aggressive investment approach.
_____ 3. Soros has tried to find good firms to invest in and to keep the stocks for many years.
_____ 4. Soros' investment style is so offensive that he is sometimes criticized.
_____ 5. Taking risks is sometimes necessary to become billionaires like the two players in finance.

Read Aloud 強く発音するところ（9か所）の○を黒く塗りつぶし，ポーズを置くところ（3か所）に／を書き入れ，CDを聞いて音読しなさい。

What you need to do is to learn how to increase your assets in a short time.
　○　　○　　　○　　　○　　○○　○　　　　○　　　　○　○　　　　○　○　　○

Information for the Topic

市場経済 (market economy)

　経済学では，市場経済は大きく3つに分類された市場で構成されていると考えます。企業が製品やサービスを家計に売る生産物市場（production market），企業が労働サービスを購入する労働市場（labor market），資金を調達するための資本市場（capital market）です。私たち個人はすべての市場に参加していますが，バフェットやソロスが活躍するのは資本市場であると言えます。

Unit 11

Grammar Section
分　詞

Grammar Points

▶ 分詞は，動詞と形容詞の性質を兼ね備えたもので，進行形や完了形に使われたり，名詞を修飾したりします。

現在分詞	動詞＋ing	A boy is **walking**.（進行形） a **walking** boy, a boy **walking** in the park（名詞修飾）
過去分詞	動詞＋ed もしくは 不規則変化	The food has been already **cooked**.（完了形） Those windows are **broken**.（受動態） **broken** windows, windows **broken** by her（名詞修飾）

▶ 分詞が動詞と接続詞の働きを兼ねて，副詞節を導くとき，その構文を分詞構文と呼びます。
　Walking along the river, I met a friend of mine.（川沿いを歩いていると友達に出会った）
　Born in Hawaii, he speaks English well.（ハワイで生まれたので彼は英語が上手だ）

Exercise 1　（　）内に入る最も適切な語句を選びなさい。

1. I was really (excited / exciting) when I earned so much money from stock sales.
2. The (rising / rose) prices in the market could not be predicted by anyone at that time.
3. The young entrepreneur is a (self-made / self-making) millionaire.
4. Working as a dealer on Wall Street must be very (fascinated / fascinating).

Exercise 2　日本語に合うように（　）内に適切な語を書き入れなさい。

1. His father was (　　　　　) to everyone as a philanthropist.
   （彼の父は慈善家としてよく知られていた）
2. His (　　　　　) attitude has been criticized by his business counterparts.
   （彼の威嚇的な態度は仕事相手からは批判されている）
3. (　　　　　) in old clothes, he didn't look like a rich businessman.
   （古い服を着ていたので，彼は金持ちのビジネスマンには見えなかった）
4. A (　　　　　) company is often made the target for investment.
   （成長している企業は，しばしば投資の対象とされる）

Exercise 3　（　）内の語を並べかえて英文を完成させなさい。

1. The consultant is always looking for (to / his / that / looks / appealing / something / clients).

2. The bank robbery (was / biggest / U.S. / the / as / history / in / reported).

3. Since (33 / been / his / by / has / cut / salary / percent), he is having a hard time making ends meet.

Unit 12 Shopping

Listening Section

Listening Tips

弱形と強形 ― **can** はいつも「キャン」と聞こえる？―

機能語には，弱く聞こえる場合（弱形）と強く聞こえる場合（強形）があります。通常，機能語は弱形で発音されますが，文末に置かれる場合や，助動詞・be 動詞などの後に省略がある場合や，強調・対比を表す場合は強形になることがあります。

1. What are you looking <u>at</u>? （強） ― I'm looing <u>at</u> the bird. （弱） ＜文末＞
2. Who <u>can</u> deliver this bed? （弱） ― Ted <u>can</u>. （強）   ＜省略＞
3. <u>Did</u> your friends deny seeing the ghost? （弱）
    ― Yes, but I <u>did</u> see it. （強）   ＜強調＞

Exercise 1 Listen to the CD and choose the statement that best describes the picture.

1. (a)　(b)　(c)　(d)　　　2. (a)　(b)　(c)　(d)

Exercise 2 Listen to the CD and choose the best response.

1. (a)　(b)　(c)　　　　　2. (a)　(b)　(c)
3. (a)　(b)　(c)　　　　　4. (a)　(b)　(c)

Exercise 3 Listen to the CD and answer the questions.

1. What product can you buy at 50% off?
    (a) Chicken pieces
    (b) Fresh fish
    (c) Frozen foods
    (d) Eggs

2. What is NOT announced as one of the supermarket's offers to customers?
    (a) Discount coupons
    (b) Wholesale prices
    (c) High-quality foods
    (d) Weekly must-buys

53

Unit 12

Reading Section
Smart Shopping

Words & Phrases 次の語句の意味を選びなさい。

1. appropriate (　)　2. occasion (　)　3. recommend (　)
4. impression (　)　5. efficient (　)　6. identity (　)
7. latest (　)　8. purchase (　)　9. tidy (　)　10. satisfy (　)

(a) 購入する　(b) 有能な　(c) 満足させる　(d) 最新の　(e) 適切な
(f) きちんとした　(g) 印象　(h) 勧める　(i) 場合　(j) 個性

次の文を読んで，後の設問に答えなさい。

Reading Passage

　Besides eating and sleeping, getting dressed is something we all do every day. It is important to wear clothes appropriate to the occasion. But with so much clothing to choose from these days, we are in danger of buying more and more, yet less and less useful items. Standing in front of a well-stocked wardrobe, you may even find that you have nothing to wear! How much do you really know about clothes shopping?

　With so much inexpensive, mass-produced clothing on the market, you can easily get lost if you don't know where to shop or what to buy. So I recommend making lists—lists of the clothes already in your wardrobe, of your must-buys, and of the things you would like to buy. Don't forget that most people you meet for the first time will judge you by what you are wearing. Your must-buys should include clothes that will make a good first impression.

　Of course, you also need to think about what casual clothing you need. People tend to think that a fashionably dressed person is an efficient person. You can find your own fashion identity by choosing from the various style choices offered by fast-fashion retailers such as UNIQLO, Forever 21, H&M, and ZARA. These shops help young people who have difficulty in keeping up with the latest fashions on a tight budget. The items on your lists, including your basic must-buys, can be purchased at minimal prices.

　We can be smarter shoppers by controlling our consumption of clothing. With a little planning, you can keep your wardrobe tidy and satisfy your desire to look fashionable at the same time. So let's all be smart shoppers and enjoy shopping!

(282 words)

in danger of ~ ～の恐れがある　well-stocked 十分物のある　retailer 小売業者
have difficulty in ~ ～に苦労する　a tight budget 厳しい予算　consumption 消費

Shopping

Exercise 1 （　）内に入る最も適切な語句を選び，文を完成させなさい。

1. The main idea of the passage is (　　).
   - (a) how to stop buying clothes
   - (b) how to avoid buying more than one needs
   - (c) how to clean out one's wardrobe
   - (d) how to keep your clothes clean
2. The word *appropriate* in line 2 means (　　).
   - (a) expensive　　(b) inexpensive　　(c) casual　　(d) suitable
3. If you (　　), shopping will become easier.
   - (a) dress up every day
   - (b) buy more and more clothes
   - (c) look well dressed
   - (d) make a list in advance
4. If you want to (　　) others, you must dress well.
   - (a) impress　　(b) meet　　(c) offend　　(d) judge
5. By (　　), fast-fashion retailers give us the choices we need to build our identity.
   - (a) purchasing at minimal prices
   - (b) deciding what people should wear
   - (c) offering a huge variety of clothing
   - (d) tightening their budgets

Exercise 2 次の各文が本文の内容に合っていればT（True），合っていなければF（False）を書きなさい。

_____ 1. Wearing whatever you want at any time is widely accepted as good manners.

_____ 2. You can have a full wardrobe and yet still do not know what to wear.

_____ 3. Most people get a first impression of somebody from what he or she says.

_____ 4. A person who wears fashionable clothing often gives the impression that he or she is irresponsible.

_____ 5. Fast-fashion retailers help young customers look well dressed on a limited budget.

Read Aloud 強く発音するところ（6か所）の○を黒く塗りつぶし，ポーズを置くところ（1か所）に／を書き入れ，CDを聞いて音読しなさい。 *T*-CD 1-85

How much do you really know about clothes shopping?
○　○　○　○　○　　○　　○　　○　　○

ℹ️ Information for the Topic

ファストファッションも着る人次第？

　セレブのファッションはマスコミの注目の的ですが，彼らがいつも高価なブランドの服を着ているわけではありません。第44代アメリカ合衆国大統領夫人のミシェル・オバマはH&Mのドレスを，イギリスのキャサリン妃はZARAの服を着用していたと報じられています。重要なのは着るものの値段ではなく，何をどのように着こなし，どのように振る舞うかというメッセージかもしれません。

55

Unit 12

Grammar Section
動 名 詞

> **Grammar Points**
>
> ▶動名詞は「動詞＋ing」で表され，通常の名詞と同じく，文の主語・目的語・補語になります。
>
> | 主語の場合 | 目的語の場合 | 補語の場合 |
> |---|---|---|
> | **Dancing** is good exercise. | He enjoyed **playing** the piano. | My hobby is **watching** TV. |
>
> ✎ 目的語に動名詞をとる主な動詞：mind, enjoy, give up, avoid, finish, escape, postpone
>
> ▶ remember や forget などの動詞は目的語が不定詞か動名詞かで意味が異なります。
> 　　Don't forget **to see** me today.（今日，私に会うことを忘れないでね）
> 　　Don't forget **seeing** me today.（今日，私に会ったことを忘れないでね）
>
> ▶「動詞＋ing」形が形容詞的に用いられた場合，それが動名詞か現在分詞か注意が必要です。
> 　　a **sleeping** bag（＝ a bag for sleeping）（寝袋）＜動名詞＞
> 　　a **sleeping** lion（＝ a lion that is sleeping）（寝ているライオン）＜現在分詞＞

Exercise 1 （　）内に入る最も適切な語句を選びなさい。

1. A shopping list will prevent you from (buy / buying / to buy) useless items.
2. My boyfriend drinks a cup of coffee while I go (shop / shopping / to shop).
3. Remember (pick up / picking up / to pick up) the ticket you booked for next week.
4. You should stop (purchase / purchasing / to purchase) things on impulse.

Exercise 2 日本語に合うように（　）内に適切な語を書き入れなさい。

1. I gave up (　　　　　) a custom-made suit because the price was extremely high for me.（私にとって極端に高価すぎたので，オーダーメイドスーツを注文するのを諦めた）
2. Some people have difficulty in (　　　　　) what they really want to wear.
（本当に着たいものを見つけることが難しい人もいる）
3. Fast-fashion retailers such as UNIQLO continue (　　　　　) young people with inexpensive clothing.
（ユニクロのようなファストファッション店は若者に高価でない商品を提供し続けている）
4. (　　　　　) a budget is important for shopping wisely in a large shopping mall.
（予算を立てることが，大きなショッピングモールで賢い買い物をするためには重要だ）

Exercise 3 （　）内の語を並べかえて英文を完成させなさい。

1. It's (asking / no / money / use / your / back / for) because it's non-refundable.

2. I (buying / vitamins / drugstore / at / forgot / some / the).

3. I (receiving / looking / jeans / am / forward / to / the) I ordered from the Internet.

Unit 13 Careers

Listening Section

Listening Tips

not の短縮形　—**can** と **can't** は聞き分けられる？—

否定を表す not は，be 動詞や助動詞の後ろに続くとき，短縮形になることがあります。be 動詞や助動詞は，肯定文では弱く短く聞こえることが多いですが，否定文で not の短縮形を含む場合は少し強く長く聞こえます。

1. They <u>were</u> available on that day.／They <u>weren't</u> available on that day.
2. She <u>has</u> set the schedule.／She <u>hasn't</u> set the schedule.
3. I <u>can</u> attend the meeting.／I <u>can't</u> attend the meeting.

Exercise 1 Listen to the CD and choose the statement that best describes the picture.

1. (a)　(b)　(c)　(d)　　　2. (a)　(b)　(c)　(d)

Exercise 2 Listen to the CD and choose the best response.

1. (a)　(b)　(c)　　　　　2. (a)　(b)　(c)
3. (a)　(b)　(c)　　　　　4. (a)　(b)　(c)

Exercise 3 Listen to the CD and answer the questions.

1. Where is this conversation probably taking place?
    (a) In a classroom
    (b) At the front desk of an office
    (c) In an interview room
    (d) In the break room

2. Why did Mr. Conway apply for the position?
    (a) He has a suitable academic background.
    (b) He thinks he can put his experience to good use.
    (c) He didn't get promoted to sales manager in his previous company.
    (d) He wants to become more flexible.

● 57

Unit 13

Reading Section
Job Hunting

Words & Phrases — 次の語句の意味を選びなさい。

1. accommodation (　)　2. qualified (　)　3. undergraduate degree (　)
4. comparable (　)　5. proficiency (　)　6. qualification (　)
7. resume (　)　8. personnel (　)　9. reliable (　)　10. evaluate (　)

(a) 履歴書　(b) 資格のある　(c) 資格・技能　(d) 同等の　(e) 堪能であること
(f) 宿泊施設　(g) 人事部（課）　(h) 信頼できる　(i) 評価する　(j) 学士号

次の文を読んで，後の設問に答えなさい。

Reading Passage

JOB OPENING: Front Desk Manager

The Sunshine Coast Hotel chain ranks among the world's most respected and most popular resort accommodations. Each year we provide over one million guests with the highest standard of service. We are seeking a highly qualified and motivated front desk manager. The applicant should have an undergraduate degree in business administration or comparable academic background. English and computer proficiency are essential. The most important qualification is the ability to manage staff to ensure maximum hospitality and guest satisfaction. For more information, please check our website. You can apply for the position by sending a copy of your resume to: personnel @schotel.com
Ms. Ginny Marshak, Director, Human Resources
Sunshine Coast Hotel

To: personnel@schotel.com
From: "Frank Groat" fgroat@xxx-yyy.com
Subject: Front Desk Manager

Dear Ms. Marshak,
I am applying for the position of front desk manager at your hotel. As you will see in the attached resume, I have the required academic qualifications as well as three years of experience working at the White Bay Resort as a front desk clerk. I have always believed that the best way to provide warm hospitality and ensure customer satisfaction is to treat guests the way that I myself would want to be treated. I think of myself as a reliable, cooperative person with excellent communication skills. While at White Bay Resort, my efforts to offer personalized service to each guest were highly evaluated and contributed in no small part to the hotel's high reputation. I would greatly appreciate your giving my resume and me your kind consideration. I am available for an interview anytime at your convenience.
Sincerely,
Frank Groat　　　　Attached File: Resume-Frank Groat.doc

(273 words)

Careers

Exercise 1 （　）内に入る最も適切な語句を選び，文を完成させなさい。

1. The main purpose of the first passage is to (　　).
   (a) inform customers of their services (b) inform employees of their benefits
   (c) advertise a job opening (d) advertise products
2. The most important qualification is (　　).
   (a) language proficiency (b) experience
   (c) staff management skills (d) an undergraduate degree
3. The resume should be (　　) the application.
   (a) revised for (b) included in (c) separate from (d) left out of
4. Mr. Groat is applying for the position because he is confident of his (　　).
   (a) English ability (b) academic background
   (c) people skills (d) computer skills
5. The word *reputation* in line 24 in the second passage means (　　).
   (a) profit (b) image (c) expense (d) burden

Exercise 2 次の各文が本文の内容に合っていればT(True)，合っていなければF(False)を書きなさい。

_____ 1. The Sunshine Coast Hotel chain needs a person whose major in college was computer science.
_____ 2. The position requires several years of practical experience.
_____ 3. Mr. Groat applied for the position by e-mail.
_____ 4. Mr. Groat has less than two years of experience working for a hotel.
_____ 5. Mr. Groat is ready to go to an interview whenever it's convenient for Ms. Marshak.

Read Aloud 強く発音するところ（6か所）の○を黒く塗りつぶし，ポーズを置くところ（1か所）に／を書き入れ，CDを聞いて音読しなさい。

We are seeking a highly qualified manager for our new hotel.
○○　○　　○○　　　　○　　　　　○　　　　　○○　　○　　　○

Information for the Topic

「社会人基礎力」を知っていますか？

　経済産業省は社会人基礎力を「職場や地域社会で多様な人々と仕事をしていくために必要な基礎的な力」として提唱しています。次の3つの能力と12の能力要素から構成されています。
「前に踏み出す力」── 主体性，働きかけ力，実行力
「考え抜く力」── 課題発見力，計画力，創造力
「チームで働く力」── 発信力，傾聴力，柔軟性，情況把握力，規律性，ストレスコントロール力

Unit 13

Grammar Section
形容詞・副詞

Grammar Points

▶ 形容詞には名詞を直接修飾する限定用法と動詞の補語として用いられる叙述用法があります。

限定用法	名詞が表す意味の範囲を限定する	I wore a **dark** dress to the party.
叙述用法	主語や目的語の状態や性質を叙述する	Let's hurry. It'll be **dark** soon.

✎ present, certain, late など，限定用法と叙述用法で意味が異なる形容詞もあります。
✎ convenient, possible, necessary などは人が主語にならない形容詞です。
   Please call on me when it is convenient for you. (× ... when you're convenient)

▶ 副詞は動詞だけでなく，形容詞・副詞・文全体などの様々な要素を修飾します。
[動詞を修飾] He spoke English **fluently** during his presentation. <様態>
[形容詞・副詞を修飾] I saw a **very** beautiful bird flying **very** fast. <程度>
[文全体を修飾] **Fortunately**, I got promoted to sales manager. <話者の心情>

Exercise 1 ( ) 内に入る最も適切な語句を選びなさい。

1. He looked (happy / happily) to be transferred to headquarters.
2. I was so (disappointing / disappointed) with my colleague's proposal.
3. The applicant tried very (hard / hardly) to make her interview successful.
4. (Are you / Is it) possible to take part in the employee training program?

Exercise 2 日本語に合うように ( ) 内に適切な語を書き入れなさい。

1. (   ) all the branches in the city had problems due to the blackout.
   (停電のために，その都市のほとんどすべての支店に問題が生じた)
2. The contract that one of our clients offered was quite (   ).
   (顧客の一社が提示した契約はとても困惑するものだった)
3. Don't drive so (   )! We still have plenty of time before the meeting.
   (そんなに速く走らないで。会議までにまだ時間がたっぷりあるから)
4. Unfortunately, the office had no conference room (   ) yesterday.
   (不運にも，昨日その事務所には利用できる会議室がなかった)

Exercise 3 ( ) 内の語を並べかえて英文を完成させなさい。

1. My elder sister (certain / that / would / succeed / was / she / in) her job search.

2. The student was (of / excited / so / get / to / employment / notification) yesterday.

3. We (a / work / little / left / order / in / to / have) complete the project.

Unit 14　Art

Listening Section

Listening Tips

be 動詞・助動詞の短縮形　—「フーズ」は **who's**？ それとも **whose**？—

主語（名詞・代名詞・疑問詞など）の後ろにくる be 動詞や助動詞は，主語に結合して短縮されることがよくあります。なかでも，is ／ has や had ／ would などは短縮形が全く同じ音になるので，話の流れや文脈で判断する必要があります。

1. It's going very well.
2. It's been a long time since we last met.
3. We'd better see the exhibition.
4. We'd like to see the exhibition.
5. Who's calling, please?
6. Whose cell phone is this?

Exercise 1　Listen to the CD and choose the statement that best describes the picture.

1.　(a)　(b)　(c)　(d)　　2.　(a)　(b)　(c)　(d)

Exercise 2　Listen to the CD and choose the best response.

1.　(a)　(b)　(c)　　　　2.　(a)　(b)　(c)
3.　(a)　(b)　(c)　　　　4.　(a)　(b)　(c)

Exercise 3　Listen to the CD and answer the questions.

1. What kind of special exhibition is being held in the museum right now?
    (a) A rich cultural heritage
    (b) Art from all over the world
    (c) Contemporary drawings and paintings
    (d) Paintings by a 20-year-old artist
2. Which statement is true about the museum?
    (a) It's open from 9 a.m. to 6 p.m. every day of the year.
    (b) It's open from 9 a.m. to 7 p.m. every day except Christmas Day.
    (c) It's open from 10 a.m. to 7 p.m. every day except New Year's Day.
    (d) It's open from 10 a.m. to 6 p.m. every day except Sunday.

Unit 14

Reading Section
The Shadow of a Great Artist

Words & Phrases ─ 次の語句の意味を選びなさい。

1. composer ( )   2. comfort ( )   3. hardship ( )   4. perform ( )
5. misfortune ( )   6. humiliation ( )   7. despair ( )
8. pursue ( )   9. struggle ( )   10. endure ( )

(a) 作曲家   (b) 演奏する   (c) 不幸   (d) 困難   (e) 耐える
(f) 慰める   (g) 絶望   (h) 屈辱   (i) 苦闘   (j) 追い求める

次の文を読んで，後の設問に答えなさい。

Reading Passage

Ludwig van Beethoven, the German composer and pianist, is one of the world's greatest musicians. In Japan, at each year's end, we hear Symphony No. 9 so often that most of us can hum the famous tune. For more than two centuries, people all around the globe have been comforted by Beethoven's creations during times of difficulty.

Almost from the moment he was born, Beethoven had to deal with overwhelming hardships. Among them, the greatest tragedy was the loss of his hearing, which began in his late twenties. Obviously, going deaf for a musician was much harder to bear than it would be for anyone else. Eventually, Beethoven became totally deaf, and was no longer able to hear his own works performed: he could hear his music only in his mind.

How did Beethoven overcome this misfortune? He described his emotional state as "humiliation," as written in his "Heiligenstadt Testament."

"... but what a humiliation for me when someone standing next to me heard a flute in the distance and I heard nothing, or someone standing next to me heard a shepherd singing and again I heard nothing. Such incidents drove me almost to despair, ... and I would have ended my life. It was only my art that held me back."

With emotional and spiritual strength, Beethoven continued to pursue his career as a great artist and didn't stop composing until he drew his final breath. His music is full of life, love, and struggle. Through his music, we can reach out to this immortal genius as a human being, a man who endured tremendous hardship for his art. Beethoven still has the great ability to delight, comfort, and encourage us.

(282 words)

Ludwig van Beethoven ルートヴィヒ・ヴァン・ベートーヴェン(1770-1827) ドイツの作曲家
Symphony No. 9 交響曲第九番　　immortal 不朽の　　tremendous すさまじい

Art

Exercise 1 （　）内に入る最も適切な語句を選び，文を完成させなさい。

1. The main idea of the passage is (　　).
    (a) Beethoven's tragedy　　　　　　　　(b) Beethoven's music
    (c) Beethoven's strength to overcome hardship　　(d) Beethoven's popularity
2. Beethoven had a difficult time because he (　　).
    (a) went blind　(b) had no close friends　(c) lost his voice　(d) went deaf
3. The word *bear* in line 9 means (　　).
    (a) to understand　(b) to endure　(c) to ignore　(d) to accept
4. (　　) was the only thing that kept Beethoven from putting an end to his life.
    (a) His family　(b) His art　(c) Humiliation　(d) Love
5. Beethoven finally stopped composing when he (　　).
    (a) passed away　　　　　　　　(b) became bored with music
    (c) lost his imagination　　　　　(d) lost his hearing

Exercise 2 次の各文が本文の内容に合っていればT(True)，合っていなければF(False)を書きなさい。

_____ 1. At the end of each year, one of Beethoven's well-known symphonies is often heard in Japan.
_____ 2. The works of Beethoven have been giving delight and comfort to people for about one hundred years.
_____ 3. The loss of Beethoven's hearing began when he was in his teens.
_____ 4. Beethoven wrote that he would have killed himself without his music to keep him going.
_____ 5. Beethoven's music never expresses his struggles and hardships.

Read Aloud　強く発音するところ（6か所）の○を黒く塗りつぶし，ポーズを置くところ（2か所）に／を書き入れ，CDを聞いて音読しなさい。

The great musician could hear his music only in his mind.
○　　○　　　○　　　　○　　　　○　　○　　　○　　　○　　　○　　○

Information for the Topic

"Heiligenstadt Testament"「ハイリゲンシュタットの遺書」

ハイリゲンシュタット（オーストリア共和国ウイーンの一部）は，進行する難聴に苦悩したベートーヴェンが療養のため訪れた場所です。その地でベートーヴェンが1802年10月6日に書いたこの遺書は，絶望の淵に立たされた心情を吐露しながらも，音楽活動に対する決意表明ともとれる内容です。その後，不屈の精神で逆境をはねのけたベートーヴェンは数多くの名曲と共に，次のような言葉も残しています。

This is the mark of a really admirable man: steadfastness in the face of trouble.
（真に称賛に値する人間の証は，困難に直面しても確固とした信念を失わないことである）

Unit 14

Grammar Section
名詞・代名詞

Grammar Points

▶ 英語の名詞には数えられる名詞（可算名詞）と数えられない名詞（不可算名詞）があります。

数えられる名詞	普通名詞	同種の人や物に共通の名を表す	dog, bus, box, dish
	集合名詞	複数の人や物の集合体を表す	people, family, audience, furniture
数えられない名詞	物質名詞	一定の区切りがない物質を表す	water, paper, money, salt
	抽象名詞	具体的な形を持たない抽象的な概念を表す	advice, information, love, knowledge
	固有名詞	特定の人や物の名を表す	Japan, Mt. Fuji, July, Tom

▶ 代名詞は同じ名詞の繰り返しを避けるためにその名詞の代わりに使われます。
　Jack bought a *piano*. — I like **it** (= the piano). ／ I want **one** (= a piano).

Exercise 1 （　）内に入る最も適切な語句を選びなさい。

1. The piano instructor gave her (a / a piece of) helpful advice.
2. Could you give me some (information / informations) on the exhibition?
3. There (was / were) a large audience in the theater.
4. This antique watch of (me / mine) was a gift from my grandfather.

Exercise 2 日本語に合うように（　）内に適切な語を書き入れなさい。

1. The (　　　　) are searching every showcase in the museum for evidence.
（警察は証拠のためにその博物館のあらゆる陳列用ケースを調べている）
2. I like this glass's design, but I don't like its color. Do you have a blue (　　　　)?
（このグラスのデザインは好きなのですが，色が気に入りません。青いのはありますか）
3. Most tickets in this shop are cheaper than (　　　　) sold at the theater box office.（この店のほとんどのチケットは劇場のチケット売り場のものよりも安い）
4. The famous musician said to his audience, "Please make (　　　　) at home and have a good time."
（その有名な音楽家は聴衆に「どうぞくつろいで楽しんでください」と言った）

Exercise 3 （　）内の語を並べかえて英文を完成させなさい。

1. A (number / of / artists / large / have / for / applied) the government grant.

2. The owner of the gallery (it / wants / look / to / stylish / more).

3. What (is / favorite / your / music / piece / of)?

Unit 15 Culture

Listening Section

Listening Tips

疑問詞の聞き取り　—5W1H はどう聞こえる？—

　疑問詞の what, when, where, why, who, how は，くだけた会話や速いスピードの自然な英語では，「ワット」，「ウェン」，「ウェア」，「ワィ」，「フ」，「ハゥ」のように聞こえることがあります。例えば，What はゆっくりと「ホワット」と聞こえるのではなく，「ワット」のように聞こえ，聞き取るのが難しいことがあります。

1. <u>What</u>?
2. <u>When</u> did you go?
3. <u>Where</u> have you been?
4. <u>Who</u> is it?
5. <u>Why</u> not answer?
6. <u>How</u> do you know?

Exercise 1　Listen to the CD and choose the statement that best describes the picture.

1. (a)　(b)　(c)　(d)　　2. (a)　(b)　(c)　(d)

Exercise 2　Listen to the CD and choose the best response.

1. (a)　(b)　(c)　　　　2. (a)　(b)　(c)
3. (a)　(b)　(c)　　　　4. (a)　(b)　(c)

Exercise 3　Listen to the CD and answer the questions.

1. What is Japan Night?
    (a) A cultural exchange program between Japan and Canada
    (b) A lecture about cultural exchanges between Japan and Canada
    (c) A cultural exchange program given by Canadian host-family members
    (d) A cultural exchange program for Canadian college students

2. When and where will Japan Night be held?
    (a) Next Sunday, in Room 113
    (b) Next Saturday, in Room 130
    (c) Next Sunday, in Room 130
    (d) Next Saturday, in Room 113

Unit 15

Reading Section
Everyday Japan and "Matsuri" Japan

Words & Phrases — 次の語句の意味を選びなさい。

1. relatively (　) 2. announcement (　) 3. remind (　) 4. concerned (　)
5. fascinate (　) 6. extreme (　) 7. collide (　)
8. contrast (　) 9. aware (　) 10. cross-cultural (　)

(a) 異文化間の　(b) 気がついている　(c) 魅了する　(d) 気づかっている　(e) 過激な
(f) 対比する　(g) 衝突する　(h) 気づかせる　(i) 比較的　(j) アナウンス

次の文を読んで，後の設問に答えなさい。

Reading Passage

　　I recently read an essay on Japanese society by an Australian woman. I found it very interesting, and it gave me a chance to think about my own country. Let me share some of her ideas with you here.

5　　The writer thinks that Japan, with its relatively low crime rate, is one of the world's safest countries. She notes that there are safety signs and announcements everywhere. One announcement reminds us not to dash for a train — even on bullet train platforms. Another warns us not to get our shoes caught in the escalator. To the writer, everyone everywhere in Japan is concerned about safety at all times. But
10　for many Japanese people, safety is something we don't really think about because we take it for granted.

　　The writer is also fascinated by Japan's "extreme" traditional festivals such as Onbashira in Suwa or the Dosojin Fire Festival in Nozawa Onsen. She sees them as dangerous because of the punching and kicking that goes on. This reminds me of the Kishiwada Danjiri (floats) Matsuri of my hometown. Danjiri teams race and
15　sometimes collide with and crash into one another. It used to be called "Kenka Matsuri."

　　In her conclusion, the writer contrasts everyday Japan with "Matsuri" Japan, and she really loves this gap. Have you ever thought about it? The title of her essay is "Japan is a very safe country with many dangerous festivals." Seeing our country
20　through the eyes of an outsider can make us aware of things we were not aware of, which is one of the many joys and benefits of cross-cultural communication.

(266 words)

Onbashira in Suwa 諏訪大社の御柱祭り（重さ10トンの巨木を山から神社まで人力のみで曳行する。途中，急坂を下ったり，川を渡ったりする）　Dosojin Fire Festival in Nozawa Onsen 野沢温泉の道祖神祭り（厄年の男たちが守る社殿に村民が火をつけようとして激しくぶつかり合う。最後は木材の社殿に激しい炎が上がる）
Kishiwada Danjiri Matsuri 岸和田だんじり祭り（「だんじり」と呼ばれる重さ4トンの地車を男たちが猛スピードで曳き，町中を疾走する。曳行路の曲がり角でも減速せずに直角に向きを変える「やりまわし」が有名）

Culture

Exercise 1 （　　）内に入る最も適切な語句を選び，文を完成させなさい。

1. "I" in the passage wants to share (　　) with readers.
   - (a) an Australian's perspective on Japanese society
   - (b) her love of festivals
   - (c) an essay on Australian tourism
   - (d) her criticisms of Japanese society

2. The Australian writer wrote that Japanese people always seem to be concerned about (　　).
   - (a) the economy
   - (b) time
   - (c) safety
   - (d) violence

3. The phrase *take it for granted* in line 10 means (　　).
   - (a) to get it without any difficulty
   - (b) to think it normal
   - (c) to make the most of it
   - (d) to worry about it

4. The Australian writer was impressed by some Japanese festivals because they seemed to her to be (　　).
   - (a) dangerous
   - (b) fashionable
   - (c) unique
   - (d) traditional

5. The Australian writer stresses the (　　) between ordinary Japanese life and some Japanese festival customs.
   - (a) similarity
   - (b) difference
   - (c) relationship
   - (d) connection

Exercise 2 次の各文が本文の内容に合っていればT (True)，合っていなければF (False)を書きなさい。

_____ 1. "I" in the passage was interested in an essay on Australian society.

_____ 2. The Australian writer notices that there are many advertising signs and announcements in Japan.

_____ 3. "I" feels that most Japanese do not really think about safety on a daily basis.

_____ 4. The Australian writer does not like Japanese festivals at all because they are too dangerous.

_____ 5. "I" concludes that cross-cultural communication gives people a chance to become more aware of their own culture and society.

Read Aloud 強く発音するところ（7か所）の○を黒く塗りつぶし，ポーズを置くところ（2か所）に／を書き入れ，CDを聞いて音読しなさい。

I recently read an essay on Japanese society by an Australian woman.

Information for the Topic

外国からのお客様

　日本政府観光局（Japan National Tourism Organization (JNTO)）によると年間の訪日外国人旅行者数は2013年12月20日に1,000万人に達しました。ただし，例年約200万人いる飛行機や船の外国人乗務員を加える新方式の集計方法ならば，すでに2007年に1,000万人を突破していました。政府は東京五輪がある2020年に，訪日客年2,000万人を達成することを新たな目標としています。

Unit 15

Grammar Section
前　置　詞

Grammar Points

▶前置詞は名詞・代名詞の前に置かれ，名詞や動詞を修飾する句を作ります。

at	時の一点（at 11 p.m.）／場所の一点（at the station）
in	時間の中（in the morning）／空間の中（in the room）／手段（in English）
on	曜日（on Monday）／日付（on March 6）／接触（on the ceiling）
for	継続期間（for two hours）／方向（for Shinjuku）／理由（for this reason）
during	特定の期間（during summer vacation）
by	近接（by my side）／期限（by the deadline）／手段（by bus）
until	継続の終了点（until [till] next month）
among	不特定多数のものの間（among college students）

✍ because of や in spite of などのように２語以上で前置詞の役割を果たすものもあります。

Exercise 1 （　　）内に入る最も適切な語句を選びなさい。

1. The international center is open (until / by / for) 9 p.m.
2. He will arrive (at / in / on) Kansai International Airport at 10 a.m.
3. There are many countries (at / in / on) Europe that I want to visit someday.
4. I enjoyed snowboarding with my friends (for / during / in) my stay in Canada.

Exercise 2 日本語に合うように（　　）内に適切な語を書き入れなさい。

1. You have to apply for the cultural exchange program (　　　　) Friday.
   （文化交流プログラムに金曜日までに申し込まなければならない）
2. According to a recent study, Japanese bonsai are very popular (　　　　) people in Asia. （最近の調査によると，日本の盆栽はアジアの人々の間で大変な人気だ）
3. The Internet enables us to read Japanese comics all (　　　　) the world.
   （インターネットのおかげで世界中で日本のコミックが読める）
4. The study abroad program was canceled because (　　　　) the flu epidemic.
   （留学プログラムはインフルエンザの流行のために中止になった）

Exercise 3 （　　）内の語を並べかえて英文を完成させなさい。

1. I was (myself / understood / trying / make / English / in / hard / to).

2. Kyoto is (for / various / its / dishes / traditional / famous).

3. Let me (you / Osaka / show / you / to / come / around / when) Japan.

Unit 16 Population

Listening Section

Listening Tips

展開を予測しながら聞く　―接続詞に注意してる？―

接続詞や接続副詞には，文章の展開を示す合図の役割があります。順接の and, then，逆接の but, however，例証を表す for example，理由を表す as, because, since，追加を表す in addition, furthermore などの接続表現に注意し，文章の展開を予測しながら聞く必要があります。

Smartphones are convenient because they have many functions. Overdependence on smartphones, however, can cause many problems. For example, smartphone addiction may keep users away from face-to-face interaction and communication.

Exercise 1 *Listen to the CD and choose the statement that best describes the picture.*

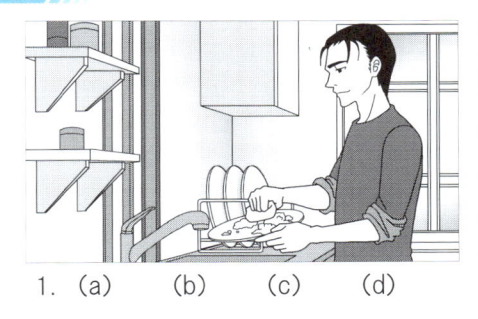

1. (a)　(b)　(c)　(d)　　　2. (a)　(b)　(c)　(d)

Exercise 2 *Listen to the CD and choose the best response.*

1. (a)　(b)　(c)　　　　　2. (a)　(b)　(c)
3. (a)　(b)　(c)　　　　　4. (a)　(b)　(c)

Exercise 3 *Listen to the CD and answer the questions.*

1. What is the main topic of the talk?
   (a) The problem of fewer children being born and its economic and social effects
   (b) The problems of an aging society and their effects on the economy and society
   (c) The measures the government has taken to solve the problem of fewer children being born
   (d) The measures the government has taken to deal with the problems of an aging society

2. Which of the following statements is NOT true?
   (a) The working population in Japan is expected to decrease in the future.
   (b) Japan's aging society will have negative effects on government spending.
   (c) Future generations may not receive sufficient social security services.
   (d) It's too late for the government to take action to deal with the aging society.

● 69

Unit 16

Reading Section
The Declining Birthrate

Words & Phrases 次の語句の意味を選びなさい。

1. birthrate ( )   2. household duties ( )   3. raise ( )
4. career-oriented ( )   5. recession ( )   6. daycare center ( )
7. social security ( )   8. childcare ( )   9. leave ( )   10. childbirth ( )

（a）出生率　（b）社会保障　（c）育児　（d）出産　（e）休暇
（f）家事　（g）不況　（h）キャリア志向の　（i）託児所(たくじしょ)　（j）育てる

次の文を読んで，後の設問に答えなさい。

Reading Passage

　Japan faces a declining birthrate crisis. This is a problem common to most developed nations, where more and more women are entering the workforce and having a hard time balancing continuing their career and their household duties, including the raising of children. But Japan's falling birthrate is especially serious, for several reasons.

　First, more and more Japanese women are getting a four-year college education. These women tend to seek career-oriented jobs, putting their work before marriage or childbirth.

　The second reason has much to do with the recent recession. An increasing number of young people have financially unstable jobs. Who wants to marry either a part-timer or a temporary contract worker who lives on a small income and faces the constant risk of being fired?

　The third factor is the shortage of daycare centers that can take care of children while the mothers are at work. If there is no one to look after their children, working mothers have no choice but to give up or postpone starting a family.

　The declining birthrate is already casting a dark shadow over Japan's social security system. That's why companies and organizations must improve their working conditions and offer more support to working mothers in various ways.

　First, companies should provide working mothers with in-house daycare centers where professional staff look after children. With such facilities located on company premises, mothers do not need to drop off and pick up their children at a daycare center. Second, companies should give longer childcare leaves, not only to working mothers, but also to their husbands, so that married couples can share the experience of childbirth and the burden (and joy) of childcare. Finally, the government should give financial support to such working-mother-friendly companies.

(288 words)

cast a dark shadow over ~　~に暗い影を落とす　　premises（建物を含む）土地，敷地
drop off ~　（乗物から）~を降ろす　　working-mother-friendly　働く母親に優しい

70

Population

Exercise 1 （　）内に入る最も適切な語句を選び，文を完成させなさい。

1. The main topic of the passage is (　　).
   (a) what to do about the increase in the number of female workers
   (b) what should be done to deal with the increase in the number of working mothers
   (c) the reasons for Japan's declining birthrate and how to solve it
   (d) what has caused the decrease in the number of married people

2. More and more working women are having difficulty in (　　).
   (a) continuing their career　(b) doing household chores
   (c) raising their children　(d) balancing their career and home responsibilities

3. Female college graduates tend to seek (　　) jobs.
   (a) short-term　(b) part-time　(c) career-oriented　(d) high-paying

4. People with financially unstable jobs find it difficult to (　　).
   (a) find a good daycare center　(b) marry a full-time worker
   (c) attract a marriage partner　(d) offer proper education to their children

5. The word *postpone* in line 15 means (　　).
   (a) call on　(b) call off　(c) put on　(d) put off

Exercise 2 次の各文が本文の内容に合っていればT(True)，合っていなければF(False)を書きなさい。

＿＿＿ 1. Among the advanced nations, Japan is the only country that is experiencing a falling birthrate.

＿＿＿ 2. One serious problem for working mothers is the shortage of daycare centers.

＿＿＿ 3. The declining birthrate is damaging Japan's social security system.

＿＿＿ 4. Giving a longer childcare leave to a husband could allow him to participate in bringing up his children.

＿＿＿ 5. The government should offer financial support to companies that offer childcare services to working mothers and fathers.

Read Aloud　強く発音するところ（7か所）の○を黒く塗りつぶし，ポーズを置くところ（2か所）に／を書き入れ，CDを聞いて音読しなさい。

Married couples can share the experience of childbirth and the burden of childcare.
○　　○　　○　　○　　○　　○　　○　　○　　○　　○　　○　　○　　○

ℹ Information for the Topic

どうする？ 少子化対策

　急速な高齢化とともに日本の将来にとって深刻なのが少子化問題です。働く母親が安心して出産や育児に取り組めるようにするには，夫や祖父母の協力が不可欠です。しかし，個人や世帯の努力には限界があります。そこで，政府や地方自治体も待機児童解消などの子育て支援策にさらに本腰を入れる必要があります。ベビーシッター体制の拡充や民間企業の保育園参入を進めるなど，官民が一体となって解決策を探る必要があります。

Unit 16

Grammar Section
接続詞

Grammar Points

▶接続詞には文法上対等の関係にある語・句・節をつなぐ等位接続詞と主節と従属節をつなぐ従位接続詞があります。

等位接続詞	語／句／節＋接続詞＋語／句／節	Tom was tired, **so** he went to bed.
従位接続詞	主節＋接続詞＋従属節	Tom went to bed **because** he was tired.

* 等位接続詞：and, but, or, yet, so
* 時と条件の従位接続詞：when, if, unless, while（while は対比を表すこともあります）
* 理由の従位接続詞：because, since, as
* 譲歩の従位接続詞：although, though, even if, even though

✎ both A and B, either A or B のように２語で成り立つ接続詞もあります。

Exercise 1 （　）内に入る最も適切な語句を選びなさい。

1. I like my job, (and / but / or) I have to quit in order to raise my child.
2. (Both / Either) my husband and I are responsible for preparing meals.
3. (If / Unless) I take a long maternity leave, it will be difficult for me to return to my workplace.
4. (Because / Even though) I have a full-time job, my husband will not help me with the housework.

Exercise 2 日本語に合うように（　）内に適切な語を書き入れなさい。

1. In the past, men worked outside, (　　　　) women stayed home and did the housework.（昔，男性が外で働き，その一方で女性は家にいて家事をした）
2. (　　　　) more and more women work outside, such a stereotyped image of marriage has changed.（外で働く女性が多くなるにつれて，そのような結婚への固定観念は変わってきた）
3. Nevertheless, my husband will say, "No way," (　　　　) I say that I want to get a part-time job.（それでも私がパートで働きたいと言えば，夫は「だめ」と言うだろう）
4. (　　　　) my son or my daughter runs errands for me when I am very busy.（私が大変忙しい時には，息子か娘のどちらかがお遣いに行ってくれる）

Exercise 3 （　）内の語を並べかえて英文を完成させなさい。

1. I waited for six months, (no / in / facilities / but / any / found / I / vacancies / childcare).

2. I can leave my office to pick up my kids in the early afternoon (my / has / flex-time / adopted / company / a / schedule / because).

3. Many women will give up having children (childcare / are / up / unless / set / centers / more).

Unit 17 Disasters

Listening Section

Listening Tips

無声音化・有声音化 —**of course** はどう聞こえる？—

声帯を震わせて発音される有声音が，声帯を震わせない無声音に変化する場合があります。例えば，of course は [v] が [f] に変化し，「オブコース」ではなく，「オフコース」のように聞こえることがあります。逆に，無声音が有声音に変化することもあります。例えば，sit up は [t] が [d] に変化し，「シットアップ」ではなく「シッダップ」のように聞こえることもあります。

1. of course
2. have to
3. a cup of tea
4. sit up
5. get out
6. what about

Exercise 1 Listen to the CD and choose the statement that best describes the picture.

1. (a)　(b)　(c)　(d) 　　2. (a)　(b)　(c)　(d)

Exercise 2 Listen to the CD and choose the best response.

1. (a)　(b)　(c)　　　　2. (a)　(b)　(c)
3. (a)　(b)　(c)　　　　4. (a)　(b)　(c)

Exercise 3 Listen to the CD and answer the questions.

1. Where is the woman?
   - (a) In a restroom
   - (b) On an escalator
   - (c) In an elevator
   - (d) On the second floor

2. How many people have been hurt?
   - (a) Four
   - (b) Five
   - (c) Six
   - (d) None

Unit 17

Reading Section
Narrow Escape

Words & Phrases 次の語句の意味を選びなさい。

1. off-shore ( )   2. crisis ( )   3. co-worker ( )   4. sustain ( )
5. lightning strike ( )   6. collapse ( )   7. ignite ( )
8. rescue operation ( )   9. commence ( )   10. dawn ( )

(a) 救助活動   (b) 危機   (c) 発火する   (d) 同僚   (e) 沖合の
(f) 夜明け   (g) こうむる (h) 雷の直撃 (i) 開始する (j) 崩壊する

次の文を読んで、後の設問に答えなさい。

Reading Passage

You are an oil engineer working for an oil company in Niigata. Several hours ago, a medium-sized typhoon, No.19, hit the Niigata coastal area. The company's head office received an emergency signal that was automatically sent from an off-shore oil rig, the *Yukiguni Ichiban*. The company has organized a crisis management team in the office. You and your co-worker, Ms. Tonomura, have been assigned a special mission to go to the company-owned oil rig, check it out, and report back on how much damage it has sustained. Ms. Tonomura is an environmental science specialist.

You and Ms. Tonomura were flying in a helicopter from Niigata to the oil rig. Some 30 minutes into the flight, the oil rig came into sight. But then, a lightning strike caused the helicopter to have serious engine trouble. The pilot lost control and had to make an emergency landing on the ocean. The impact damaged the helicopter, but nobody was injured. You have managed to launch a life raft with survival kits aboard.

Part of the oil rig has collapsed, and oil leaking from it has already been ignited by sparks from batteries. Now the damaged helicopter is sinking. Oil is spreading from it towards you and may catch fire at any time. You are in extreme danger! The pilot was able to send out an SOS message. The rescue team knows your position, but the rescue operation won't commence until dawn. The ocean current is moving northward. You have survival kits and must try to escape from harm's way!   (256 words)

<The list of contents of a survival kit>
1. compass 2. flash light 3. mirror 4. paddle
5. generator (20kg) 6. rice balls 7. 60m strong nylon rope
8. briefcase 9. bottled water 10. diving suits

oil rig 石油掘削装置   launch 海面におろす   life raft 救命ボート   emergency landing 不時着水
survival kit 緊急時用品   ocean current 海流

Disasters

Exercise 1 （　）内に入る最も適切な語句を選び，文を完成させなさい。

1. The company is trying to solve the problem after receiving an emergency (　　).
   (a) exit　　　　(b) supplies　　　(c) signal　　　(d) landing
2. The word *mission* in line 6 means (　　).
   (a) attempt　　(b) accident　　　(c) volunteer work　(d) job
3. The pilot had (　　) to make an emergency landing on the ocean.
   (a) great skill for　　　　　　　(b) no choice but
   (c) no idea how　　　　　　　　(d) a lot of trouble
4. You are now at (　　) on the map after making an emergency landing.
   (a) point Ⓐ　　(b) point Ⓑ　　　(c) point Ⓒ　　(d) point Ⓓ
5. The rescue team received information about your (　　) upon receiving an SOS message.
   (a) voice message　　　　　　　(b) life raft
   (c) code number　　　　　　　　(d) present position

Exercise 2 次の各文が本文の内容に合っていればT(True)，合っていなければF(False)を書きなさい。

_____ 1. The company asked you and your co-worker to examine the damaged oil rig.
_____ 2. It took about an hour and a half to go by helicopter from Niigata to the oil rig.
_____ 3. The life raft with the survival kits was launched from the damaged helicopter.
_____ 4. The leaked oil from the oil rig caught fire after the collapse.
_____ 5. The rescue team started their operation before the sun rose.

Read Aloud 強く発音するところ（7か所）の○を黒く塗りつぶし，ポーズを置くところ（2か所）に／を書き入れ，CDを聞いて音読しなさい。 *T* CD 2-35

You have survival kits and must try to escape from harm's way!
○　○　　○　　○　　○　　　○　○　　○　　○　○　　○

ⓘ Information for the Topic

地球温暖化の影響

　気候変動に関する政府間パネル（IPCC: Intergovernmental Panel on Climate Change）のコンピューターモデルは2080年までに海水面が1メートル上昇する可能性を示唆しています。このまま温暖化が進めば，北極・南極の氷が溶け出して，海岸地帯の低地が水没する危険性があります。さらに巨大台風の出現，集中豪雨や竜巻などの異常気象により，大災害の頻発が懸念されています。

●75

Unit 17

Grammar Section
いろいろな否定

Grammar Points

▶ 否定表現には，大きく分けて 2 つの意味的な種類があります。

全体否定	「(全く)～ない」のように文の表す内容全体を否定するもの。	I have **not** read the article.
部分否定	「いつも～とは限らない」のように文の表す内容の一部だけを否定するもの。	My father is **not** always free on Sundays.

▶ not を用いずに，特定の語や構文でも否定を表すことができます。
　Nobody tells the truth.（誰も本当のことを言っていない）
　There is **little** water in the bottle.（ボトルの中にはほとんど水がない）
　I can **hardly** understand what he says.（私は彼の言うことがほとんど理解できない）
　Who knows?（誰が知っているだろうか [=誰も知らない]）

Exercise 1 （　）内に入る最も適切な語句を選びなさい。

1. The pilot could (not / ever) control the helicopter due to engine failure.
2. We can (no / never) predict when an earthquake will occur.
3. (Nobody / All) has experienced such a strong earthquake in the last 100 years.
4. (Whose / Who) has ever seen a tsunami wipe out a whole town before?

Exercise 2 日本語に合うように（　）内に適切な語を書き入れなさい。

1. (　　　　　) of the train passengers were injured in the crash.
   （列車の衝突でほとんどの乗客は負傷しなかった）
2. The cause of a tsunami is not (　　　　　) an earthquake or strong wind.
   （津波の原因はいつも地震や強風とは限らない）
3. Your solution for escaping from this danger is (　　　　　) from perfect.
   （危機から脱出するための君たちの解決策は完璧にはほど遠い）
4. (　　　　　)(　　　　　) of the skiers on the slope were killed in the snow slide.（雪崩でゲレンデにいたスキーヤー全員が死亡したわけではない）

Exercise 3 （　）内の語を並べかえて英文を完成させなさい。

1. I (seen / terrible / a / have / disaster / such / never) before.
   _____

2. Japan (hit / always / by / powerful / isn't / typhoon / a) every year.
   _____

3. The rescue team (hard / had / starting / operation / a / time / their) because of the fire.
   _____

Unit 18 Travel

Listening Section

Listening Tips

まぎらわしい音 —**light** と **right** は聞き分けられる？—

[l] と [r]，[b] と [v] などの子音を含む語の中には，発音が似ているため日本人にとって区別して聞き取ることが難しい類音語があります。似た音の語を聞き分けるには，文脈なども手がかりにして音の違いを正しく聞き取る必要があります。

1. light – right
2. glass – grass
3. load – road
4. best – vest
5. boat – vote
6. ban – van

Exercise 1 Listen to the CD and choose the statement that best describes the picture.

1. (a) (b) (c) (d)   2. (a) (b) (c) (d)

Exercise 2 Listen to the CD and choose the best response.

1. (a) (b) (c)   2. (a) (b) (c)
3. (a) (b) (c)   4. (a) (b) (c)

Exercise 3 Listen to the CD and answer the questions.

1. Where is the announcement probably taking place?
   (a) In a train station
   (b) In a bus
   (c) In a hotel lobby
   (d) In a train

2. How long will the tourists spend at the Sapporo Clock Tower?
   (a) One hour
   (b) Two hours
   (c) Three hours
   (d) Four hours

Unit 18

Reading Section
Invitation to Hokkaido

Words & Phrases — 次の語句の意味を選びなさい。

1. destination (　)　　2. guarantee (　)　　3. outstanding (　)
4. hot-air balloon (　)　　5. enchant (　)　　6. extraordinary (　)
7. crab (　)　　8. flavor (　)　　9. second to none (　)　　10. ski resort (　)

(a) スキー場　　(b) 熱気球　　(c) 魅了する　　(d) 特徴づける　　(e) 並はずれた
(f) かに　　(g) 保証する　　(h) 何にも劣らない　　(i) 目的地　　(j) すばらしい

次の文を読んで，後の設問に答えなさい。

Reading Passage

　Most people travel to relax and enjoy life. Hokkaido, Japan's large northern island, is a great tourist destination because there's no place quite like it in all of Japan. Beautiful scenery is guaranteed—no matter what time of year you visit. And Hokkaido, with its wide-open spaces, gives a feeling of freedom that you can't get anywhere else in the country.

　Hokkaido has many outstanding views of nature. Take a ride in a hot-air balloon and you will be enchanted with the extraordinary beauty of the scenery. Many areas such as Kushiro Shitsugen and Lake Mashu are in their original pristine state.

　If you like delicious fresh food, especially seafood, Hokkaido is the place for you. It has all kinds of fantastic restaurants. Some serve a traditional Mongolian mutton barbecue called "Jingisukan." Others specialize in fresh crab. Hokkaido also has some of the best sushi in the world. And in a robata-yaki restaurant, you can watch as chefs roast tasty local foods by the fireside.

　Hokkaido is also the home of the Ainu people, and some Ainu culture still flavors the island. A large number of place names originated from the Ainu language. Ainu museums are available if you want to learn about local culture.

　Hokkaido is also a great place to enjoy skiing. The snow quality and slope conditions are second to none. Major ski resorts attract hundreds of thousands of skiers annually, including many foreigners who love Hokkaido's high-quality snow. Nowadays, believe it or not, foreign real estate agents are buying land and houses in Hokkaido for skiers from overseas.

　Local Resident
　　Minoru Shiragata

(266 words)

originate from ~ 〜に由来する　　real estate agent 不動産屋

Travel

Exercise 1 （　）内に入る最も適切な語句を選び，文を完成させなさい。

1. You can enjoy wonderful scenery (　　) in Hokkaido.
   (a) in winter　　(b) in spring and fall
   (c) in summer　　(d) all year round
2. The word *pristine* in line 8 means (　　).
   (a) colorful　　(b) fresh　　(c) normal　　(d) beautiful
3. "Jingisukan" is the name of a traditional (　　) barbecue that is popular in Hokkaido.
   (a) deer　　(b) beef　　(c) mutton　　(d) pork
4. Many (　　) in Hokkaido come from the Ainu language.
   (a) place names　　(b) local customs　　(c) tourist areas　　(d) family names
5. Many skiers from overseas come to Hokkaido for (　　).
   (a) the land and houses　　(b) the Ainu culture
   (c) the high-quality snow　　(d) hot-air balloons

Exercise 2 次の各文が本文の内容に合っていればT(True)，合っていなければF(False)を書きなさい。

_____ 1. Hokkaido is no longer the popular destination for travelers that it once was.
_____ 2. Hokkaido's wide-open spaces are unique in Japan.
_____ 3. Local chefs in robata-yaki restaurants prepare dishes by the fireside.
_____ 4. Nothing is left of Hokkaido's Ainu culture and language.
_____ 5. Hokkaido's slopes and snow make it a popular destination for overseas ski enthusiasts.

Read Aloud 強く発音するところ（8か所）の○を黒く塗りつぶし，ポーズを置くところ（2か所）に／を書き入れ，CDを聞いて音読しなさい。 *T-CD 2-42*

A lot of ski resorts attract hundreds of thousands of skiers annually.
○　○　○　○　　○　　　○　　　　○　　　　○　　　　　○　　○　○

Information for the Topic

北海道の地名に残るアイヌ文化

　納沙布，新冠，長万部，これらの地名が読めますか。それぞれ，「ノシャップ」，「ニイカップ」，「オシャマンベ」と読みます。実はアイヌ語の地名に漢字を当てているのです。このような地名が北海道には数多くあります。アイヌ人は狩猟民族で，土地の形状などが想像できるネーミングをしていると言われています。例えば，小樽は「砂がたくさんある場所」，札幌は「乾いた広い土地」という意味です。「北海道」は明治時代に日本人が付けた名前です。アイヌ語では北海道を「アイヌモシリ」と呼びます。「アイヌ」とは「人間」という意味で，「アイヌモシリ」は「人間が住む静かな土地」という意味です。

Unit 18

Grammar Section
名詞構文・無生物主語構文

Grammar Points

▶「動詞／形容詞（＋副詞）」が表す内容は「（形容詞＋）名詞」でも表現することができます。

動詞／形容詞（＋副詞）を用いた表現	（形容詞＋）名詞を用いた表現
Mary **swims** very well.	Mary is a very good **swimmer**.
Did you know that Tom had **arrived**?	Did you know about Tom's **arrival**?
I noticed that he was **absent** from the class.	I noticed his **absence** from the class.

▶日本語では人間または生物を主語とするほうが自然な文でも，英語では無生物を主語にして表現することがよくあります。

　　This movie will give you a good idea of what life in Japan today is like.
　　（この映画があなたに現在の日本の生活がどのようなものか想像を与えるでしょう）（直訳）
　　（この映画を見れば，あなたは現在の日本の生活がどのようなものか想像できるでしょう）（意訳）

Exercise 1 （　　）内に入る最も適切な語句を選びなさい。

1. She makes an excellent tour guide for foreigners because she is such a good （speaking / speaker）of English.
2. The storm prevented me from（taking / take）a trip to the Big Island of Hawaii.
3. Tokyo Sky Tree（makes / offers）us an excellent view of Tokyo.
4. （What / Why）makes you so happy? – I'm leaving for Canada tomorrow.

Exercise 2 日本語に合うように（　　）内に適切な語を書き入れなさい。

1. I didn't have a good (　　　　　) last night because of jet lag.
   （時差ボケで，昨夜はよく眠れなかった）
2. He works as a scuba diving instructor since he is such a good (　　　　　) himself.
   （彼は優れた潜水夫なので，スキューバダイビングのインストラクターとして働いている）
3. This cruise will (　　　　　) you a good chance to make new friends.
   （この船旅に参加すれば，新しく友だちを作るチャンスがあります）
4. The Internet (　　　　　) us to shop for the cheapest flights.
   （インターネットで格安航空券が買える）

Exercise 3 （　　）内の語を並べかえて英文を完成させなさい。

1. We changed（the / of / plans / late / our / arrival / because）of the plane.
   _____

2. We will soon（decision / a / travel / plane / whether / make / to / by）or by train.
   _____

3. This photograph（Australia / of / pleasant / me / journey / reminds / to / our）ten years ago.
   _____

Unit 19　Sports

Listening Section

Listening Tips

数量表現 I　—「42.195」はどう聞こえる？—

数字は文字で見れば一目瞭然ですが，音声で聞き取ることは容易ではありません。それぞれの数量表現の正しい読み方を確認し，実際の会話では発音の違いやアクセントの位置などに注意して，正確に聞き取る必要があります。

1. 19
2. 90
3. 365
4. 127,817,277
5. 42.195
6. 2/3
7. 2 : 3
8. 3 + 5 = 8

Exercise 1　Listen to the CD and choose the statement that best describes the picture.

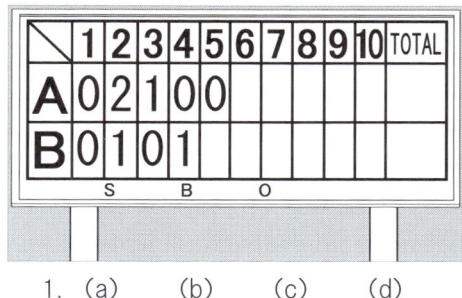

1. (a) 　(b) 　(c) 　(d)　　2. (a) 　(b) 　(c) 　(d)

Exercise 2　Listen to the CD and choose the best response.

1. (a) 　(b) 　(c) 　　　　2. (a) 　(b) 　(c)
3. (a) 　(b) 　(c) 　　　　4. (a) 　(b) 　(c)

Exercise 3　Listen to the CD and answer the questions.

1. What does the woman want to do?
    (a) To tour the fitness center
    (b) To get in shape
    (c) To do some aerobics
    (d) To buy a bathing suit

2. Which exercise is the woman going to do?
    (a) Weight training
    (b) Treadmill
    (c) Stationary bike
    (d) Swimming

● 81

Unit 19

Reading Section
The World's Most Popular Sport?

Words & Phrases ——次の語句の意味を選びなさい。

1. major ( )　2. candidate ( )　3. association ( )　4. participate ( )
5. trend ( )　6. equipment ( )　7. opponent ( )
8. survey ( )　9. foundation ( )　10. enormous ( )

(a) 協会　　(b) 用具　　(c) 主要な　　(d) 財団　　(e) 候補
(f) 膨大な　(g) 流行　　(h) 調査　　　(i) 競争相手　(j) 参加する

次の文を読んで，後の設問に答えなさい。

Reading Passage

　What is the world's most popular sport? The best way to answer this question is probably to examine the "player population" of each sport region by region.

　In Japan, there is no question that baseball and soccer are the two major candidates for the most popular sport. Considering only the number of players
5　registered in sports associations around the country, baseball (including "rubber-ball" baseball) is Japan's largest sport, with over 1.2 million players. Soccer comes in second with about 880,000 players. Basketball ranks third with 616,000 players, and volleyball comes in fourth with 429,000 players.

　Globally, however, basketball is said to have the largest player population.
10　According to the International Basketball Federation, at least 450 million players play "hoops" around the world. Surprisingly, this is almost twice the number of soccer players registered in the Federation Internationale de Football Association. At about 250 million players, soccer, then, is only a distant second, but still far ahead of baseball, with only 35 million participating in games worldwide.

15　These days, a lifestyle emphasizing fitness is becoming more important, and regular exercise has become a global trend among health-conscious people. Walking is the most prevalent form of exercise. No equipment, no teams, no opponents are needed, and people of both sexes and all ages can take part. A survey by a Japanese foundation even suggests that walking is the most popular *sport* in
20　Japan, with over 23 million participants a year. If we recognize walking as a kind of sport, then the total number of walkers worldwide would be enormous!

(257 words)

region by region 地域ごとに　　there is no question ~ 〜は間違いない　　rubber-ball baseball 軟式野球
International Basketball Federation 国際バスケットボール連盟　　play "hoops" バスケットボールをする
Federation Internationale de Football Association 国際サッカー連盟
distant second 1位と大差のある2位　　health-conscious 健康志向の

Sports

Exercise 1 (　　) 内に入る最も適切な語句を選び，文を完成させなさい。

1. The best way to find out the world's most popular sport is to examine (　　).
   (a) its history　　　　　　　　(b) the number of fans
   (c) the number of players　　　(d) the ticket sales

2. Taking player population into consideration, Japan's most popular sport is (　　).
   (a) baseball　　(b) basketball　　(c) soccer　　(d) volleyball

3. It is said that (　　) has the largest player population in the world.
   (a) baseball　　(b) basketball　　(c) soccer　　(d) volleyball

4. The word *fitness* in line 15 means the condition of being physically (　　).
   (a) attractive　　(b) powerful　　(c) slim　　(d) healthy

5. Walking has become very popular around the world because (　　).
   (a) it is not at all tiring　　　　(b) it requires no effort
   (c) it burns the most fat　　　　(d) it does not require a lot of equipment

Exercise 2 次の各文が本文の内容に合っていれば T (True)，合っていなければ F (False) を書きなさい。

_____ 1. Soccer is considered to be the number one sport in Japan.

_____ 2. In Japan, volleyball is more popular than basketball.

_____ 3. There are almost twice the number of basketball players as there are soccer players in the world.

_____ 4. Globally, baseball is not as popular as it is in Japan.

_____ 5. More and more people are walking for exercise these days because it is good for all ages and both sexes.

Read Aloud
強く発音するところ（8 か所）の○を黒く塗りつぶし，ポーズを置くところ（3 か所）に／を書き入れ，CD を聞いて音読しなさい。

Globally, however, basketball is said to have the largest player population.

ℹ Information for the Topic

クリケットが世界第3位！?
　競技人口の算定は，用いられる資料に限りがあるため，その正確な数字を把握することは困難です。そんな中，クリケットがバスケットボール，サッカーに次ぐ世界第3位の競技人口を持つスポーツだとする調査もあります。クリケットにあまり馴染みのない日本人にとってはいささか驚くべき結果ですが，世界で2番目に人口の多いインドをはじめ，南アフリカやオーストラリアなどの旧イギリス植民地で大人気のクリケットが世界第3位の人気スポーツだとしてもそれほど不思議ではないのかもしれません。

Unit 19

Grammar Section
比較表現Ⅰ：原級・比較級・最上級

Grammar Points

▶ 2つ以上のものを比較して表現するときは形容詞・副詞の原級・比較級・最上級を用います。

原　級	A is as＋原級＋as B.	Mr. Yamada is **as tall as** Mr. Tanaka.
比較級	A is＋比較級＋than B.	Mr. Suzuki is **taller** than Mr. Yamada.
最上級	A is the＋最上級＋of [in] B.	Mr. Suzuki is **the tallest** of the three.

✍ 比較級や最上級を強めるには much, far, by far などを形容詞・副詞の前に置きます。

▶ 形容詞・副詞の規則変化には，原級の語尾に -er, -est を付けるものと原級の前に more, most を置くものがあります。また，不規則変化するものや変化が複数あるものもあります。
　規則変化：fast – faster – fastest, beautiful – more beautiful – most beautiful
　不規則変化：good / well – better – best, bad / ill – worse – worst, little – less – least
　比較級・最上級が2つあるもの：late – later / latter – latest / last

Exercise 1 （　）内に入る最も適切な語句を選びなさい。

1. My new tennis partner is (more / most / best) skilled than my old one.
2. For athletes, practice is the best instructor (in / of / than) all.
3. Basketball is (very / much / the) more popular than volleyball in Japan.
4. Tiger Woods is one of the (good / better / best) golfers in the world.

Exercise 2 日本語に合うように（　）内に適切な語を書き入れなさい。

1. Most amateur teams are (　　　　) poor (　　　　) a church mouse.
　（ほとんどのアマチュアチームは教会のネズミのように貧しい）
2. Which do you like (　　　　), skiing or snowboarding?
　（スキーとスノーボード，どっちがより好きですか）
3. From a global perspective, baseball players are paid (　　　　) than soccer players.（世界的に見れば，野球選手の給料はサッカー選手より少ない）
4. Top athletes actively put the (　　　　) technology into practice.
　（一流のアスリートは最新の技術を積極的に練習に取り入れます）

Exercise 3 （　）内の語を並べかえて英文を完成させなさい。

1. The figure skater (the / far / performance / gave / worst / of / by) her career.

2. Nothing (more / of / than / a / water / is / drink / refreshing) after exercise.

3. He (as / the / coach / as / any / good / in / a / is) league.

Unit 20　Life

Listening Section

Listening Tips

数量表現 II　―特別な数字はどう聞こえる?―

　数字は私たちの日常生活に深く関わっており，読み方に特別なルールがあるものも多く存在します。郵便番号，番地，時刻，日付，西暦，金額，温度，面積など，それぞれの数量表現の正しい読み方に慣れる必要があります。

1. 443-0507　　2. 22-B Baker Street　　3. 10:15 a.m.　　4. July 4
5. in 2008　　6. $10.15　　7. 26℃　　8. 100㎡

Exercise 1　Listen to the CD and choose the statement that best describes the picture.

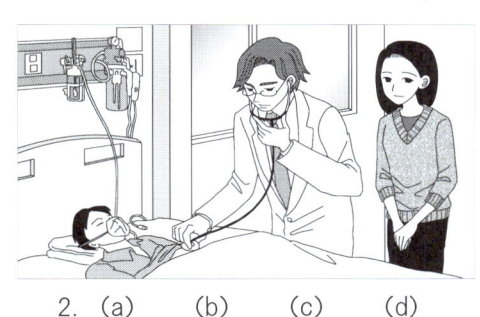

1.　(a)　(b)　(c)　(d)　　　　2.　(a)　(b)　(c)　(d)

Exercise 2　Listen to the CD and choose the best response.

1.　(a)　(b)　(c)　　　　2.　(a)　(b)　(c)
3.　(a)　(b)　(c)　　　　4.　(a)　(b)　(c)

Exercise 3　Listen to the CD and answer the questions.

1. When was the woman hit by the car?
    (a) At around 9:00 p.m.
    (b) At around 10:00 p.m.
    (c) At around 11:00 p.m.
    (d) At around midnight

2. What is anyone who witnessed the incident asked to do?
    (a) Visit the injured woman in the hospital
    (b) Telephone the police department
    (c) Identify the injured woman
    (d) Visit the police station in person

● 85

Unit 20

Reading Section
Quality of Life

Words & Phrases 次の語句の意味を選びなさい。

1. debate (　)　　2. consciousness (　)　　3. ventilator (　)
4. breadwinner (　)　5. right (　)　6. suspect (　)
7. extent (　)　8. ethical (　)　9. ignore (　)　10. perspective (　)

(a) 人工呼吸器　(b) 疑う　(c) 倫理的な　(d) 権利　(e) 無視する
(f) 議論・討論　(g) 見通し・観点　(h) 意識　(i) 大黒柱　(j) 程度

次の文を読んで，後の設問に答えなさい。

Reading Passage

　When a person is suffering from cancer or other serious illness, and there is no hope of recovery, a debate arises as to whether that person should be kept alive or should be allowed to die.

　Kentaro, 50, fell into a coma after a car accident. Although the doctors managed to save his life, they had to tell his family there was no hope that he would ever regain consciousness. He was being kept alive on a life-support ventilator. Since Kentaro was the family breadwinner, it was clear that his family would have serious money problems and a mental burden on their shoulders if he were kept alive.

　Some relatives advised his wife to ask the doctors to remove the ventilator. They insisted, "Kentaro is in a vegetative state with no possibility of recovery—it's meaningless to continue treatment." Other relatives, however, said, "We are of course sad to see you having such a hard time, but Kentaro has a right to live."

　One doctor at a Sapporo hospital is suspected of allowing a patient to die by removing the patient's life support. This incident has raised questions over the extent to which doctors should provide patients with life-sustaining treatment. The main question is where to draw the line between necessary and excessive treatment.

　No matter how many limits we set, some ethical problems will remain. We cannot ignore the patients' suffering or the emotional burden of their families. Of course, the patients should not be pressured by their families into choosing death. As our society ages, this problem will become more serious. We should thus consider the quality of life from the perspective of everyone involved in these sad situations.

(281 words)

fall into a coma 昏睡状態に陥る　　vegetative state 植物人間の状態　　life- sustaining 生命維持の

Life

Exercise 1 （　　）内に入る最も適切な語句を選び，文を完成させなさい。

1. When a patient has (　　) of recovering from cancer or other serious illness, a debate comes up.
   (a) a chance　　(b) a mental burden　　(c) emotional problems　　(d) no hope

2. The phrase *regain consciousness* in lines 5~6 means to become (　　) what is happening again.
   (a) unclear about　　(b) interested in　　(c) aware of　　(d) bored with

3. Kentaro was able to survive with the help of (　　).
   (a) a life-support ventilator　　(b) volunteers　　(c) surgery　　(d) donations

4. There were two different (　　) among Kentaro's relatives about his medical treatment.
   (a) memories　　(b) suspicions　　(c) supports　　(d) opinions

5. It is not easy to decide whether to continue medical treatment, because (　　).
   (a) it may cause doctors to give up
   (b) it may cause the hospital money problems
   (c) there is no clear line between necessary and excessive treatment
   (d) everyone is too sad to think clearly

Exercise 2 次の各文が本文の内容に合っていればT(True), 合っていなければF(False)を書きなさい。

_____ 1. If a person becomes seriously ill, his/her family has the right to decide everything about his/her medical treatment.

_____ 2. Kentaro lost consciousness after being involved in a car accident.

_____ 3. Everyone in Kentaro's family was against removing his life support.

_____ 4. Both the patients' suffering and the burden of the family should be taken into account when patients are in a hopeless condition.

_____ 5. It is becoming increasingly important in our aging society for us to think about the quality of life.

Read Aloud 強く発音するところ（6か所）の○を黒く塗りつぶし，ポーズを置くところ（2か所）に／を書き入れ，CDを聞いて音読しなさい。

The patients should not be pressured by their families into choosing death.
○　○　　　○　　○　○　　○　　　　○　　　○　○　　　○　　○　　○

ℹ Information for the Topic

Quality of Life (QOL)

　QOLとは，どれだけ人間的に豊かな生活ができるかを指標にした考え方です。医療分野では患者の生活の質のことを指します。最近では，病院などの医療機関を中心にして，日常生活行動を回復させるだけではなく，食事も，温かい食べ物は温かくして提供するなどの工夫がなされています。趣味なども含め，患者が望むQOLをいかに向上させるかに関心が集まっています。

Unit 20

Grammar Section
比較表現Ⅱ：いろいろな比較表現

Grammar Points

▶「AはBの〜倍（分の1）…だ」という倍数表現を作るときは形容詞・副詞の原級を，「AはBの中で〜番目に…だ」という序列表現を作るときは最上級を用います。

倍数表現	A is ＋ 倍数／分数 ＋ as ＋ 原級 ＋ as B.	Susan is **twice as** tall **as** Mary.
序列表現	A is the ＋ 序数 ＋ 最上級 ＋ of [in] B.	He is **the third tallest** boy in the club.

▶そのほかにも比較表現を用いた重要構文があります。

Speak **as** slowly **as** you **can**. (= Speak **as** slowly **as possible**.)
He is **not so much** a teacher **as** a scholar. (= He is a scholar **rather than** a teacher.)
The younger you are, **the easier** it is to learn a foreign language.
Tokyo is becoming a **more and more** popular place to visit.
You must read **at least** one book a month.

Exercise 1　(　) 内に入る最も適切な語句を選びなさい。

1. Do you really want to live as long as you (can / possible)?
2. I would rather die tomorrow (as / than) be kept alive in a vegetative state.
3. Can a life with technology be (twice / second) as happy as one without it?
4. The more you think about life, (the / much) less you understand it.

Exercise 2　日本語に合うように (　) 内に適切な語を書き入れなさい。

1. Sierra Leone has only about (　　　　) as long an average life expectancy as Japan.（シエラレオネの平均寿命は日本の半分ほどしかない）
2. In Japan, pneumonia is (　　　　)(　　　　) largest killer after heart disease.（日本では，肺炎が心疾患に次いで3番目に大きい死因である）
3. (　　　　) and (　　　　) genetic information has become available recently.（近年，ますます多くの遺伝情報が手に入るようになってきている）
4. It will cost (　　　　)(　　　　) 100 million yen for her son to undergo surgery.（彼女の息子が手術を受けるには少なくとも1億円はかかるだろう）

Exercise 3　(　) 内の語を並べかえて英文を完成させなさい。

1. Life is (as / much / a / position / not / of / matter / so) of disposition.

2. Humans (do / times / much / as / work / as / ten / monkeys).

3. The older she gets, (more / she / the / terrified / is) of death.

Unit 21 Entertainment

Listening Section

Listening Tips

知っているつもりの英語　—**towel** はどう聞こえる？—

　日本語にはたくさんの外国語由来の語が「カタカナ言葉」として定着しています。その中には，日本語としてはよく知っているのに，英語としての発音を理解していないために音と意味が結びつきにくい語もあります。そのような"知っているつもり"の英語を聞き取るには，何よりも正しい発音の知識が必要です。

1. towel　　　2. bucket　　　3. tunnel　　　4. iron
5. sweater　　6. oasis　　　　7. virus　　　　8. theme

Exercise 1　Listen to the CD and choose the statement that best describes the picture.

1. (a)　(b)　(c)　(d)　　　　2. (a)　(b)　(c)　(d)

Exercise 2　Listen to the CD and choose the best response.

1. (a)　(b)　(c)　　　　　　2. (a)　(b)　(c)
3. (a)　(b)　(c)　　　　　　4. (a)　(b)　(c)

Exercise 3　Listen to the CD and answer the questions.

1. Which show are they going to see?
   (a) *Les Miserables*
   (b) *Aladdin*
   (c) *Mamma Mia!*
   (d) *The Lion King*

2. What will the woman do next?
   (a) Change their plans for the weekend
   (b) Go to the box office
   (c) Check an Internet website
   (d) Call a theater

Unit 21

Reading Section
Television Prime Time

Words & Phrases — 次の語句の意味を選びなさい。

1. programming ( )   2. rating ( )   3. define ( )   4. exact ( )
5. slightly ( )   6. conventionally ( )   7. traditionally ( )
8. vitality ( )   9. diversification ( )   10. advent ( )

(a) 正確な   (b) 慣習的に   (c) 登場   (d) 定義する   (e) わずかに
(f) 活力   (g) 視聴率   (h) 伝統的に   (i) 多様化   (j) 番組制作

次の文を読んで，後の設問に答えなさい。

Reading Passage

　Prime time is the block of time for TV programming that comes during the middle of the evening. It refers to the time period in which the most popular shows are screened and the highest ratings are achieved.

　The term *prime time* is often defined in terms of a fixed time period, but the exact range differs slightly from country to country. For example, in Japan, prime time (also known as *golden time*) conventionally covers the time slot from 7:00 p.m. to 11:00 p.m. In the U.S., prime time traditionally runs from 8:00 p.m. to 11:00 p.m., from Monday to Saturday. On Sundays, it begins an hour earlier.

　The programming content in prime time also varies between the two countries. In Japan, regular programs such as news shows, variety shows, dramas, and movies are the most popular shows during prime time. In the U.S., situation comedies (or *sitcoms*), reality shows, and dramas are the most frequently watched. Some channels air reruns of older, "classic" shows during prime time.

　For the TV industry, prime time ratings are an important index that indicates the vitality or success of each broadcast station. But average ratings for prime time have been declining recently. One reason is the diversification of media that has come with the advent of the Internet. Another big reason is the development of video-on-demand technology, which enables us to watch our favorite programs anytime we want. In the near future, the time period that we call *prime time* may become a thing of the past.

(254 words)

screen（TVなどで）放送する　　from country to country 国によって　　situation comedy ホームコメディー　reality show リアリティー番組（役者が演じるドラマではなくて，一般人の現実の様子やプライバシーを撮ったホームビデオで構成される低予算のテレビ番組）　　rerun 再放送　　video-on-demand technology ビデオ・オン・デマンド技術

Entertainment

Exercise 1 （　）内に入る最も適切な語句を選び，文を完成させなさい。

1. Prime time usually refers to the time period on TV in which (　　) are broadcast.
   (a) the most serious programs　　(b) breaking news programs
   (c) family-only programs　　(d) the highest-rated programs
2. In Japan, *prime time* is also called (　　).
   (a) silver time　　(b) golden time　　(c) high time　　(d) peak time
3. In the U.S., prime time normally starts at (　　).
   (a) 6:00 p.m.　　(b) 7:00 p.m.　　(c) 8:00 p.m.　　(d) 9:00 p.m.
4. The word *classic* in line 13 means (　　).
   (a) unique　　(b) superior　　(c) romantic　　(d) typical
5. One of the reasons for declining prime time ratings is (　　).
   (a) the advent of high-tech computers　　(b) the low quality of TV programs
   (c) the global economic slump　　(d) video-on-demand technology

Exercise 2 次の各文が本文の内容に合っていればT(True)，合っていなければF(False)を書きなさい。

_____ 1. While prime times are the same in all countries, the content is different.
_____ 2. In the U.S., prime time starts an hour earlier on Sundays.
_____ 3. In Japan, situation comedies and reality shows are the most popular programs during prime time.
_____ 4. Dramas are very popular both in Japan and in the U.S. during prime time.
_____ 5. Prime time ratings in all countries will most likely remain at the same level in the years to come.

Read Aloud 強く発音するところ（10か所）の○を黒く塗りつぶし，ポーズを置くところ（4か所）に／を書き入れ，CDを聞いて音読しなさい。

Prime time is the block of time for TV programming that comes during the middle of the evening.

Information for the Topic

高視聴率の条件は？

　価値観や娯楽が多様化した現代では，大勢の人が同じ時間帯に同じTV番組を視聴するという機会は減りました。それでも日本のNHK紅白歌合戦や米国のスーパーボウル中継（アメリカンフットボールの優勝決定戦）は例年40％以上の高視聴率を記録しています。最近では，2014年の「FIFAワールドカップ・日本×コートジボワール」が46.6％という高視聴率を記録しました。どうやら高視聴率の条件は，みんなが観たいと思うことはもちろん，その番組が独占生中継であることが大きいようです。

Unit 21

Grammar Section
関係詞 I：関係代名詞

Grammar Points

▶ 関係代名詞は接続詞と代名詞の機能を併せ持ち，2つの文を1つにまとめることができます。
　She is a teen idol. + She has many fans. ⇒ She is a teen idol [**who** has many fans].

▶ 関係代名詞は先行詞の種類や関係節内での文法的機能によっていくつかの種類があります。

先行詞の種類	主格	所有格	目的格
人	who	whose	whom
人以外	which	whose	which

✎ 主格と目的格の関係代名詞は that で代用できます（先行詞に最上級や only などの強調表現が含まれる場合は that が優先されます）。目的格の関係代名詞は省略が可能です。

▶ what は先行詞を含む関係代名詞で，文の主語・目的語・補語となる名詞節を導きます。
　I can't believe **what** (= the thing that) he says.（彼の言うことは信用できない）

Exercise 1　( ) 内に入る最も適切な語句を選びなさい。

1. The other day I saw a Broadway musical, (who / which / whose) I found very entertaining.
2. I have a friend (who / whom / whose) mother is a famous opera singer.
3. Tom has three daughters, all of (whose / whom / them) are fashion models.
4. That was the only movie (what / who / that) I saw last year.

Exercise 2　日本語に合うように ( ) 内に適切な語を書き入れなさい。

1. He has a large collection of miniature cars, the total value of (　　　　) can't be overestimated.（彼はミニカーを多数集めているが，その合計価値は計り知れない）
2. At the airport I ran into a popular child actress (　　　　) talent I admire.
（私は空港でその演技の才能に感心している人気の子役女優に偶然出くわした）
3. I don't like going out to karaoke with someone (　　　　) has no ear for music.
（私は音痴の人とカラオケに行くのが嫌いです）
4. Such time-wasting forms of entertainment are (　　　　) really make some teachers angry.（そのような時間を無駄にする娯楽は実際に一部の教師を怒らせるものです）

Exercise 3　( ) 内の語を並べかえて英文を完成させなさい。

1. I enjoyed talking (to / sat / man / to / the / whom / I / next) at the concert.

2. There (the / in / was / interested / that / little / program / very) me.

3. What (a / entertainment / is / need / you / in / more / little) your life.

Unit 22 Language

Listening Section

> **Listening Tips**
>
> 通じているつもりの英語 ―war はどう聞こえる?―
>
> すでに知っている英単語でも日本語式に発音すると通じないことがあります。war のようにローマ字の綴りと発音が異なる語、major などの語に含まれる二重母音、bell のように「ゥ」「ォ」に聞こえる語末の [l]、little, mountain, sudden のような語末の音には注意が必要です。また、strong のように母音が挿入されない子音連結にも注意が必要です。
>
> 1. award　　　2. meter　　　3. potato　　　4. milk
> 5. bottle　　　6. certain　　7. struggle　　8. strength

Exercise 1 Listen to the CD and choose the statement that best describes the picture.

1. (a)　(b)　(c)　(d)　　2. (a)　(b)　(c)　(d)

Exercise 2 Listen to the CD and choose the best response.

1. (a)　(b)　(c)　　　　2. (a)　(b)　(c)
3. (a)　(b)　(c)　　　　4. (a)　(b)　(c)

Exercise 3 Listen to the CD and answer the questions.

1. What is the main topic of the talk?
   (a) Japanese people like to shorten English words in a uniquely Japanese way.
   (b) Not all foreign loanwords come from English.
   (c) Japanese who use loanwords often cannot make themselves understood in English for several reasons.
   (d) The more loanwords Japanese use when speaking in English, the better their ability to communicate.

2. Which of the following statements is true?
   (a) Native speakers of English understand most loanwords despite their Japanized pronunciation.
   (b) Some loanwords like *pasokon*, though abbreviated in a Japanese way, make sense in English.
   (c) Knowing the origins of loanwords enables learners to use them correctly.
   (d) Loanwords should be avoided because they can cause miscommunication.

Unit 22

Reading Section
Loanwords in Japanese

Words & Phrases 次の語句の意味を選びなさい。

1. loanword (　) 2. excessive use (　) 3. controversy (　)
4. enrich (　) 5. lexicon (　) 6. come into being (　)
7. influx (　) 8. civilization (　) 9. equivalent (　) 10. abuse (　)

(a) 乱用　　(b) 豊かにする　(c) 文明　　(d) 同等物／同等の　(e) 論争
(f) 流入　　(g) 生まれる　　(h) 借用語　(i) 過度の使用　　　(j) 語彙目録

次の文を読んで，後の設問に答えなさい。

Reading Passage

　An elderly man in Gifu Prefecture sued Japan's major broadcasting station for causing him mental distress over the station's excessive use of *gairaigo* (loanwords from foreign languages written in katakana). Although the local court refused to hear the case, it is easy to see why such loanwords are difficult to understand for
5 elderly people who are not familiar with them. Thus, the elderly man's complaint renewed a controversy over the use of loanwords in the Japanese language.
　The entry of loanwords into a language is not limited to Japanese, of course. English has enriched its vocabulary by adding many foreign words from Latin, Greek, and mostly French to its lexicon. Loanwords come into being when two cultures
10 come into contact. A language borrows a word when it doesn't have a word of its own to describe a new thing or concept. This explains the huge influx of Western-based foreign words into Japanese during the Meiji Period (1868-1912). It was an era when the Japanese imported and borrowed many new things and ideas from Western civilization, for which there were no equivalents in Japan.
15 　The debate over katakana loanwords is not, however, about words that have been traditionally used as part of the Japanese lexicon, words such as *news*, *stress*, *sports*, and *volunteer*. Rather, the problem is the abuse of loanwords, that is, the excessive or unnecessary use of such words, for which good words already exist in Japanese. For example, today we find too many katakana words in the media, words like *gabanansu*
20 (governance), *ameniti* (amenity), *akauntabiriti* (accountability), and *konpuraiansu* (compliance). Why do you use loanwords in situations where there are equivalent Japanese words? Many people would agree that the recent trend has gone too far; they say it is having a negative effect on the Japanese language. What do you think?

(302 words)

sue 提訴する　　local court 地方裁判所　　renew 新たにする　　go too far 行き過ぎる

94

Language

Exercise 1 （　）内に入る最も適切な語句を選び，文を完成させなさい。

1. This passage discusses the issue of (　　) of loanwords.
   (a) the incorrect use　(b) the overuse　(c) the underuse　(d) the importation
2. The word *distress* in line 2 refers to something that causes you to feel (　　).
   (a) foolish　　　(b) shy　　　(c) pleased　　　(d) worried
3. Loanwords spelled in katakana are especially difficult for (　　) to understand.
   (a) children　　(b) teenagers　　(c) country people　(d) elderly people
4. In general, loanwords have (　　) effects on a language.
   (a) only positive
   (b) only negative
   (c) both positive and negative
   (d) neither positive nor negative
5. The passage is against the use of loanwords as a substitute for Japanese words that have a (　　) meaning.
   (a) different　　(b) familiar　　(c) original　　(d) similar

Exercise 2　次の各文が本文の内容に合っていればT(True)，合っていなければF(False)を書きなさい。

_____ 1. The elderly man's complaint changed the broadcasting station's policy.
_____ 2. Not only Japanese but English has borrowed many loanwords from foreign languages.
_____ 3. The Japanese language borrowed many Western-based foreign words during the Meiji Era.
_____ 4. The author of the passage considers words such as *news*, *stress*, *sports*, and *volunteer* to be examples of problematic loanwords.
_____ 5. The media use too many loanwords for which there are good Japanese equivalents.

Read Aloud　強く発音するところ（7か所）の○を黒く塗りつぶし，ポーズを置くところ（1か所）に／を書き入れ，CDを聞いて音読しなさい。 *T*.CD 2-70

Loanwords come into being when two cultures come into contact.
○　　　　○　　○　　○　　　○　　　○　　○　　　　○　　○　　○

Information for the Topic

和製英語に注意！

カタカナで表される外来語には，元の英単語と発音だけでなく，意味も異なる語が多くあります。例えば，「カンニング」の元の語である cunning は「名ずるさ，狡猾さ，形ずるい，狡猾な」という意味で，「(試験中の) 不正行為」を表す語は cheating になります。また，「スマホ」(smartphone) や「アプリ」(application; 英語での省略形は app) などのように日本語式に省略された語を英語として使用しても通じませんので注意しましょう。

Unit 22

Grammar Section
関係詞 II：関係副詞

Grammar Points

▶ 関係副詞は接続詞と副詞の機能を持つ語で，先行詞の意味によって where, when, why, how の4種類があります。

where	先行詞が「場所」	I remember the place **where** you were born.
when	先行詞が「時」	I remember the day **when** we first met.
why	先行詞が「理由」	Tell me the reason **why** you were late.
how	先行詞が「方法」	Tell me **how** you solved the problem.

✍ 関係副詞を用いた文では，先行詞の省略が可能です。
✍ 方法を表す how の場合は，先行詞か関係副詞かのどちらか一方のみを用います。
　（× Tell me the way **how** you solved the problem.）

Exercise 1 （　）内に入る最も適切な語句を選びなさい。

1. I visited a primary school (which / where / how) the children are learning French.
2. Do you know (when / which / who) the English language underwent its most dramatic changes?
3. Tell me the reason (where / why / how) you are studying Russian.
4. Tell me (who / which / how) you were able to make such an excellent translation of Japanese folktales into English.

Exercise 2 日本語に合うように（　）内に適切な語を書き入れなさい。

1. Many loanwords date back to the Meiji Era (　　　　) Japanese came into contact with Westerners.（多くの借用語の起源は日本人が西洋人と接触した明治時代に遡る）
2. I went to an international school (　　　　) many subjects were taught only in English.（私は多くの教科が英語のみで教えられるインターナショナルスクールに通った）
3. I don't understand (　　　　) your child has become trilingual so quickly.（あなたの子供がどのようにしてそれほど早く3か国語を話せるようになったのかわからない）
4. I will explain the reasons (　　　　) English has become an international language.（なぜ，英語が国際語になったのかという理由について説明します）

Exercise 3 （　）内の語を並べかえて英文を完成させなさい。

1. I will (seven / acquired / you / how / I / languages / have / tell).

2. I was brought up in (where / spoken / a / many / country / languages / are).

3. The day will soon (machine / will / accurate / when / translation / be / come / and) dependable.

Unit 23 Science

Listening Section

Listening Tips

アメリカ英語の特徴 I　―water はどう聞こえる？―

アメリカ英語のくだけた会話や速いスピードの会話では，water などの語中（単語の語頭と語末以外）の [t] の音が変化し，「ウォーター」というよりも，「ウォダー」や「ウォラー」のように聞こえることがあります。イギリス英語では「オニオン」のように発音する音声を，アメリカ英語では「アニアン」のように発音されることがあります。このような発音の違いにも注意が必要です。

1. <u>Water</u>, please.
2. Pre<u>tt</u>y good.
3. See you <u>later</u>.
4. I don't like <u>onions</u>.
5. Put it in the <u>box</u>.
6. A cup of <u>coffee</u>, please.

Exercise 1 Listen to the CD and choose the statement that best describes the picture.

1. (a)　(b)　(c)　(d)
2. (a)　(b)　(c)　(d)

Exercise 2 Listen to the CD and choose the best response.

1. (a)　(b)　(c)
2. (a)　(b)　(c)
3. (a)　(b)　(c)
4. (a)　(b)　(c)

Exercise 3 Listen to the CD and answer the questions.

1. Where is the conversation probably taking place?
    (a) At the library next to the main entrance
    (b) In a science classroom
    (c) On the way to the campus bus stop
    (d) In the parking lot

2. Which topic will the woman write about?
    (a) General science
    (b) Nanotechnology
    (c) iPS cells
    (d) The change in the number of the planets

Unit 23

Reading Section
The Goal of Science

Words & Phrases 次の語句の意味を選びなさい。

1. prove ( )　　2. predict ( )　　3. phenomenon ( )　　4. theory ( )
5. practice ( )　　6. innovation ( )　　7. solar ( )
8. dwarf planet ( )　　9. definition ( )　　10. delete ( )

(a) 技術革新　　(b) 太陽の　　(c) 実践　　(d) 理論　　(e) 定義
(f) 準惑星　　(g) 削除する　　(h) 現象　　(i) 予言する　　(j) 証明する

次の文を読んで，後の設問に答えなさい。

Reading Passage

　In science, old facts are replaced by new facts once the new facts are proved valid. Scientists observe, explain, and predict real-world phenomena to come up with better theories and practices. Scientific discoveries and innovations should be useful for everyday life. If science had not existed, we would still be living in a cave using tools made of stone.

　In the history of science, there have been many great scientists who have discovered scientific truths: Copernicus, Newton, Einstein, to name a few. Copernicus put the sun at the center of the solar system, Newton explained the law of universal gravitation, and Einstein gave us the theory of relativity. What would science be like today if it had not been for their breakthroughs?

　Recently, another great scientific change came about. Traditionally there were nine planets in the solar system: Mercury, Venus, Earth, Mars, Jupiter, Saturn, Uranus, Neptune, and Pluto. But after Eris, one of the dwarf planets, was discovered by Mike Brown in 2005, the definition of a planet was changed, and the number of planets became eight, with Pluto being deleted from the list. This is just another example of a new fact replacing an old one.

　So what is the goal of science? Scientists must continue to try to find true facts that can be used to solve difficult problems such as global warming and pollution. Science should make our lives convenient, fruitful, and better.

(236 words)

Copernicus コペルニクス(1473-1543) ポーランドの天文学者　　Newton ニュートン(1642-1727) 英国の自然哲学者で数学者　　Einstein アインシュタイン(1879-1955) ドイツの理論物理学者　　to name a few 少し例をあげると　　the law of universal gravitation 万有引力の法則　　the theory of relativity 相対性理論　　Uranus 天王星　　Neptune 海王星　　Pluto 冥王星　　Mike Brown マイク・ブラウン(1965-) 米国の天文学者

Science

Exercise 1 （　　）内に入る最も適切な語句を選び，文を完成させなさい。

1. The most important thing for scientists is to try to discover facts (　　).
   (a) that will be interesting   (b) that will be mysterious
   (c) that will be true   (d) that will be profitable

2. The model of the solar system with the sun at the center was discovered by (　　).
   (a) Copernicus   (b) Einstein   (c) Newton   (d) Brown

3. The word *breakthroughs* in line 10 means (　　).
   (a) facts   (b) theories   (c) trials   (d) discoveries

4. The number of planets at present is eight because (　　) was deleted from the list.
   (a) Eris   (b) Mars   (c) Pluto   (d) Venus

5. The number of planets was reduced because our ideas about (　　) changed.
   (a) how a planet is made   (b) how a planet is defined
   (c) how far away a planet is   (d) how fascinating a planet is

Exercise 2 次の各文が本文の内容に合っていればT(True)，合っていなければF(False)を書きなさい。

_____ 1. Scientific discoveries and innovations have nothing to do with everyday life.

_____ 2. The development of science has enabled us to live outside the cave.

_____ 3. Newton discovered the law of universal gravitation.

_____ 4. Eris, which was discovered by Mike Brown, was soon added to the list of planets, bringing the total to eight.

_____ 5. We can use new scientific discoveries to help us solve some environmental problems such as global warming and pollution.

Read Aloud 強く発音するところ（8か所）の○を黒く塗りつぶし，ポーズを置くところ（2か所）に／を書き入れ，CDを聞いて音読しなさい。

Without science, we would still be living in a cave using tools made of stone.
　○　　　○　　　　○　○　　　○　○○　　　○　○　○　○　　　○　　　○　○

ℹ Information for the Topic

「科学である」ということ

　ある事象が「科学である」と認められるには，その事象が常に真実であることが証明されなければなりません。ある事象が科学であると証明されれば，100%その事象が起こることになります。したがって，科学を我々の日常生活に応用する時には十分注意する必要があります。また，科学を否定するには，たった一つでも真実ではない例外を挙げることができればよいことになります。

Unit 23

Grammar Section
仮定法Ⅰ：仮定法過去・仮定法過去完了

Grammar Points

▶現在や過去の事実に反する内容を仮定して表現するときは仮定法を用います。

仮定法過去 （現在の事実に反する 内容を述べる）	［条件節］If＋主語＋動詞（過去形）… ［帰結節］主語＋would/could/might＋動詞… If I **were** a bird, I **could** fly to you.
仮定法過去完了 （過去の事実に反する 内容を述べる）	［条件節］If＋主語＋had＋過去分詞… ［帰結節］主語＋would/could/might＋have＋過去分詞… If you **had come** to the party, you **could have met** him.

▶未来の起こりそうにない出来事を仮定する場合は，条件を表す if 節に should を用います。
　If anyone **should** come, tell him I'm out.（万一誰か来たら，不在だと伝えてください）

Exercise 1 （　）内に入る最も適切な語句を選びなさい。

1. The world's forests (could be / could have been) saved if the 3 Rs were followed.
2. If DNA (was not / had not been) discovered, Dolly would not have been cloned.
3. If you (should / will) win the Nobel Prize, you would be respected by many people.
4. I'll tell you as soon as possible if I (see / saw) a shooting star in the sky tonight.

Exercise 2 日本語に合うように（　）内に適切な語を書き入れなさい。

1. If experiments were more fun, more children (　　　　　) like science.
　（もし実験がもっと楽しかったら，もっと多くの子供達が科学を好きになるでしょう）
2. If rockets (　　　　　) not been developed, man could not have landed on the moon.（もしロケットが開発されていなければ，人類は月に着陸できなかったでしょう）
3. If I (　　　　　) more about programming languages, I would try to develop better computer programs.
　（もっとプログラム言語を知っていたら，より良いコンピュータープログラムを開発してみたい）
4. If scientists (　　　　　) to find the explanation for the Big Bang, a great mystery would be solved.（科学者がビッグバンの原因を突き止めていたら，その謎は存在しないだろう）

Exercise 3 （　）内の語を並べかえて英文を完成させなさい。

1. If (harder / studied / had / a / mathematics / she / little), she could have been a scientist.

2. If science had not progressed in the past, (living / might / be / a / we / caves / in) even now.

3. If Darwin had not written *On the Origin of Species*, (known / have / the / would / about / theory / not / we) of evolution.

Unit 24 Technology

Listening Section

> **Listening Tips**
>
> **アメリカ英語の特徴 II ― want to go はどう聞こえる？―**
>
> アメリカ英語のくだけた会話や速いスピードの会話では，want to go の発音が「ワナゴゥ」のように聞こえることがあります。また，twenty, let me, give me もそれぞれ「トゥエニィ」，「レミ」，「ギミ」のように聞こえることがあります。このようなアメリカ英語の特徴には注意が必要です。
>
> 1. I <u>want to go</u> there.　　2. I'm <u>going to</u> do it.　　3. I worked for <u>twenty</u> hours.
> 4. <u>Let me</u> introduce myself.　　5. <u>Give me</u> a break.

Exercise 1 Listen to the CD and choose the statement that best describes the picture.

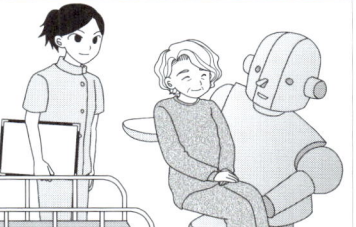

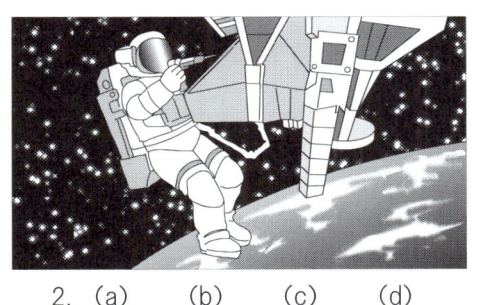

1. (a)　(b)　(c)　(d)　　2. (a)　(b)　(c)　(d)

Exercise 2 Listen to the CD and choose the best response.

1. (a)　(b)　(c)　　　　2. (a)　(b)　(c)
3. (a)　(b)　(c)　　　　4. (a)　(b)　(c)

Exercise 3 Listen to the CD and answer the questions.

1. What is the main topic of the lecture?
    (a) Mobile phones for banking use in Africa
    (b) Various educational uses for mobile phones in Africa
    (c) The United Nations' goals for mobile phone development
    (d) Improving education for girls and women in Africa

2. Which of these is NOT mentioned as an aspect of daily life that uses mobile phones as a communication tool?
    (a) health
    (b) politics
    (c) crime
    (d) farming

Unit 24

Reading Section
A Language Robot

Words & Phrases 次の語句の意味を選びなさい。

1. sophomore (　)　2. aid (　)　3. work on (　)　4. advance (　)
5. carry out (　)　6. correspond to (　)　7. angle (　)
8. trial and error (　)　9. function (　)　10. convert (　)

(a) 変換する　(b) 向上させる　(c) 見地・角度　(d) 〜に取り組む　(e) 達成する
(f) 機能する　(g) 補助する　(h) 試行錯誤　(i) 大学二年生　(j) 〜に相当する

次の文を読んで，後の設問に答えなさい。

Reading Passage

　Many learners of a foreign language wish they could study abroad with a "language robot." Yoshio is a sophomore who has that dream and who is now studying **Introduction to Computer Science**. In that course, students are asked to do a research project on how to use computer technology to improve or aid the human brain. Yoshio has been interested in developing computer programs for several years. Now, he is working on making a robot that understands and writes spoken English. In other words, the robot listens to a series of English sounds as input and then it writes English sentences as output.

　Deeper understanding of human language and more advanced computer technology skills are required for this project. Without advanced computer technology, a language robot could not be developed. To carry out this project, we need computer programs that can copy man's language processing systems. In other words, we need to understand language acquisition (how we learn language) and must be able to program a computer. A language robot must include basic systems such as listening, thinking, and writing, with each system corresponding to human ears, brains, and hands, respectively.

　After looking at the problem from all angles, Yoshio suddenly realizes that he has no idea how to get the robot's hand to move to write sentences. So he decides to ask one of his friends who knows a lot about human body movements to help him. Yoshio realizes something else: a period of trial and error will be needed until the robot can function well enough to do language jobs.

　Yoshio learns that thinking about language robots can show us how complex our use of language is and how difficult it is to convert language systems to computer programs. But he also learns that it's possible to develop an excellent language robot—as long as we do our homework.

(311 words)

language acquisition 言語の獲得

Technology

Exercise 1 （　　）内に入る最も適切な語句を選び，文を完成させなさい。

1. The main purpose of the passage is (　　).
   (a) to describe 'Computer Science' course
   (b) to demonstrate how to write a research project
   (c) to explain what it takes to develop a language robot
   (d) to explain advanced computer technology

2. Yoshio is a (　　) university student.
   (a) first-year　　(b) second-year　　(c) third-year　　(d) fourth-year

3. The word *aid* in line 4 means (　　).
   (a) analyze　　(b) enlarge　　(c) assist　　(d) explain

4. (　　) is/are responsible for the mental function of language acquisition.
   (a) The brain　　(b) The ears　　(c) The hands　　(d) Body movements

5. A period of (　　) must be gone through to make sure the language robot functions well.
   (a) input and output　　　　(b) language acquisition
   (c) step by step　　　　　　(d) trial and error

Exercise 2　次の各文が本文の内容に合っていればT(True)，合っていなければF(False)を書きなさい。

_____ 1. Yoshio is a graduate student with an interest in computer science.
_____ 2. Yoshio is planning to design a language robot.
_____ 3. The robot Yoshio is making can already speak and write English.
_____ 4. A language robot would be able to do programmed activities related to human language.
_____ 5. Yoshio has all the knowledge and skills he needs to develop a working language robot.

Read Aloud　強く発音するところ（6か所）の○を黒く塗りつぶし，ポーズを置くところ（2か所）に／を書き入れ，CDを聞いて音読しなさい。　*T*-CD 2-84

He has been interested in developing computer programs for several years.
○　○　○　○　　　　○　○　　　　　○　○　　　○　○　　　○

Information for the Topic

言語ロボットの可能性

　言語ロボットの開発には，言語を構成している①語彙，文法，意味等のメカニズム，②文法に語を挿入した結果を意味として解釈するプロセス，③個々の音声特徴，語のアクセント，文のイントネーション等を言語プログラムにする必要があります。基本的には0と1の組み合わせである言語プログラムとして人間の言語表現をどの程度まで記述することが可能でしょうか。また，言語ロボットに必要不可欠であるコンピューター技術は，人間の言語を充分に表現できるまで向上する可能性を秘めているのでしょうか。

●103

Unit 24

Grammar Section
仮定法Ⅱ：いろいろな仮定表現

Grammar Points

▶仮定法には，if 節を用いた構文のほかにも次のような慣用表現があります。
I wish I could travel around the world.（世界旅行にいけたらなあ）
She sang **as if** she were a professional singer.（彼女はまるでプロ歌手のように歌った）
Without air, we could not live.（空気がなければ，私たちは生きられないだろう）
A true teacher **would** not use such a word.（真の教師なら，そのような言葉は使わない）
Suppose you were in my place, what would you do?（私の立場だったらどうしますか）
I ran to the bus stop; **otherwise**, I would have missed my bus.
（私はバス停まで走った。そうでなければ，バスに乗り遅れていただろう）

Exercise 1 （　　）内に入る最も適切な語句を選びなさい。

1. I wish I (will know / knew) more about the role of technology in society.
2. (With / Without) modern technology, we would not be developing self-driven cars.
3. The latest powerful telescopes (otherwise / could) make out the shapes of stars more clearly.
4. (Suppose / With) you were the leader of the project, what would you like to design?

Exercise 2 日本語に合うように（　　）内に適切な語を書き入れなさい。

1. I would not assemble the robot like that, if I (　　　　　) you.
   （もし私があなただったら，そのようにロボットを組み立てないでしょう）
2. Taro talked (　　　　　)(　　　　　) he knew everything about artificial intelligence.（太郎は，人工知能についてあらゆることを知っているかのように話した）
3. Hi-tech computers (　　　　　) be able to tell us the exact time earthquakes will happen.（高度なコンピュータだったら，地震が来る正確な時を予測することができるでしょう）
4. There were excellent engineers working on Jack's team; (　　　　　), he could not have won the car race.
   （優れた技術者がジャックのチームで働いていなければ，ジャックはカーレースで勝てなかっただろう）

Exercise 3 （　　）内の語を並べかえて英文を完成させなさい。

1. Suppose (computers / wrote / you / for / programs), what programs would you write?

2. I (could / developed / I / have / wish) more user-friendly e-learning programs.

3. To listen to Taro's presentation, you (all / he / had / think / the / would / conducted) experiments by himself.

Appendix

英語らしい音声をもとめて

1　はじめに

　グローバル世界のコミュニケーション手段として必要不可欠である英語を聞いたり，話したりする力を向上させるために，文レベルの音声特徴，ポーズ，英語のリズム，語が連続する場合に生じる音声特徴について学びます。さらに，数字の読み方，日本語化した英語，米語の音声特徴等も学び，初級レベルの英語の音声特徴を身につけます。各 Unit の Listening Tips を参考にしながら説明いたします。

2　日本人英語の音声特徴

　日本人が英語の発音を向上させるには，日本語と英語の音声特徴を比較しながら，英語の音声を聞き，英語らしく話す訓練をすることが効果的です。ここでは日本人英語の音声特徴の代表として二つの例について考えます。

　最初は，日本語の基本的な音声単位が，子音（C）＋母音（V）であるために生じる英語の連続する子音に母音を挿入してしまう発音です。英語の street の初めの部分は，C(s)+C(t)+C(r)- のように子音が3個連続して発音されますが，初級レベルの日本人英語学習者の発音が，[sutori-] のように発音されて，英語の [str-] とは異なった発音になることがあります。このように子音の連続する英語の発音を身につけるには，scrambled を練習してみてください。母音の前に3個の子音，後ろに4個の子音が連続している発音ができれば，あらゆる英語の子音連続の発音に対応できます。このような音声が連続している scrambled (eggs) を [sukur+æ+m(u)buludo] のような日本語式の発音ではなく [skr+æ+mbld] のように英語らしく発音できるようになれば英語の子音連続が身についたことになります。

　次に that の発音を日本語的な発音から，英語らしい発音に変える方法を考えてみましょう。多くの日本人の英語学習者は，that の発音が日本語の音声とは異なる事実はよく知っていてその訓練もよくしています。しかし，that が文の中で異なった使われ方をする場合の音声の長さや強さを理解した上で，that を聞いたり話したりしている人はあまり多くはありません。

　　例1　Can you see *that*?
　　例2　I admit *that* I did it.

例1の that は，例2の that に比較して強く長く発音されます。日本人英語学習者は，初級，中級，上級になるに従って，例2の that の長さが例1に比較して短くなっていき，native speakers に近づいていくことがわかっています。例1の that は，「ザット」と強く長く発音されるのに対して，例2の that は，「ザッ」と弱く短く発音されます。例2の that の長さと強さを例1の that の約3分の1の長さと強さにすると native speakers の英語の発音に近づけることができます。

3　英語の文

　英語の文に使われている語には，Unit 1 に示されているようにその働きによって強く長く発音される語（内容語）と弱く短く発音される語（機能語）があります。従って，英語の文を読んだり話したりするためにはこのような特徴を意識して訓練することが大切です。例3を英語らしく発音するためには，次のような点に気を付けて練習します。

例3　I graduated from high school in March / and I am a college student now.
　　　・　●(・)(・)　　・　　●　　　●　　　・　　●　・　●(・)　●(・)　●
　　　　　　　　　　　　　　　　　　　　　　　　　　(本テキストでは，(・)は表記なし)

小さな丸(・)は弱く短く発音し，大きな黒丸(●)は強く長く発音します。このテキストでは，内容語に相当する強く長く発音する語には一つの●をつけていますが，実際は語には音節単位で強く長く発音するところと弱く短く発音するところがあります。例3の文に使用されている語では，次のようになります。

　　　graduated　　　　　college　　　　student
　　　●・・　　　　　　　●・　　　　　●・

また，例3では，high school が同じ強さで示されています(●●)が，実際は強く発音するところも2段階の強さに分けるのが普通です。例えば，the White House (米国大統領官邸：名詞[一語扱い])は，●●のように発音され，white house (白い家：形容詞＋名詞[二語])は，●●のように発音されます。音声の弱い部分も com-mu-ni-ca-tion の初めの部分の発音に見られるようにcom-mu- の部分が・●のように二段階に区別されて発音されます。語全体の発音は・●・●・となります。英文で例示すると次のようになります。

例4　Mr. White was an English teacher who taught English as a means of
　　　●　　●　　・・　●　　●　・　(・)　●　(・)　●　(・)　・・　●
　　　communication.
　　　(・)　(●)(・)●(・)

従って，音声の強弱は四段階にするのが一般的ですが，このテキストでは，強(●)と弱(・)の二つに区別しています。その理由は，日本語の音声特徴であるほぼ同じ強さの音声を続けて英語を発音する傾向（クリスマス；●●●●●）から，英語本来の発音に近づくためには，最初に，強弱(●・)の区別を理解した上で，次第により多くの種類の音声の強弱の変化を訓練してほしいからです。ほぼ同じ強さの音声を続けて発音する傾向のある日本語式リズムはマシンガンタイプリズムとかスタッカートリズムとか呼ばれています。日本語的なリズムを英語のリズムに変化させるには，強弱のあるリズムに変化させることがポイントです。英語らしいリズムで発音できたら，文を読む時や英語を話す時に意味のまとまりで息をつく（ポーズ[／]で示す）ようにするとさらに英語らしくなります。このような発音ができるようになると，英語を聞く時にも，ポーズとポーズの間で意味がまとまっていることが理解でき，効果的にリスニングできるばかりでなく，話す英語がより通じるようにもなります。

また，英語の文を読む時には，Unit 3に示してあるイントネーションにも注意する必要があります。平叙文や疑問詞のある疑問文は下降調で，疑問詞のない疑問文は上昇調，未完結の文は水平調で読むことが原則です。

実際話されている英語には，さまざまな音声のパターンが見られます。疑問文の形でなくても，Pardon?(↗)のように上昇調に発音すれば，相手の言った情報を確認することになります。また疑問文でも，音調により話し手の意図が異なる場合があります。What did you say?(↘)と下降調で発音すれば，相手の返答の内容を聞くことになります。同じ英文でも，What did you say?(↗)と上昇調で発音すると，話の内容を聞き返して確認することになります。選択疑問文としてAかBかを尋ねる時には，Which do you like better, baseball(↗) or football?(↘)のように，Aは上昇調(↗)，Bは下降調(↘)になります。付加疑問文においては，You like English, don't you?(↗)では相手に返答を求め，You like English, don't you?(↘)では相手の言ったことを確認する違いが

107

あります。平叙文で複数のものを列挙する時には，I like apples,(↗) oranges,(↗) and melons.(↘) のように列挙が続く時には上昇調(↗)で列挙が終わる時には下降調(↘)になります。また文を話す時や聞く時に注意すべき音声的な特徴として，文の中で強勢が置かれる語や句が問われている情報によって変わるということです。I went to the concert with John by train yesterday. という文で考えると，強勢を置かれる可能性は次のようになります。(a)–(f)で聞かれている内容に応じて英文の(1)–(6)の語句に強勢が置かれます。

例5 **I went to the concert** with **John** by **train yesterday**.
　　　(1)　(2)　　　(3)　　　(4)　　(5)　　(6)

(a) **Who** went to the concert yesterday?　　(b) **What did you do** yesterday?

(c) **Where** did you go yesterday?　　(d) **Who** did you go to the concert with?

(e) **How** did you go to the concert with John yesterday?

(f) **When** did you go to the concert with John?

4　英語のリズム

英語のリズムは日本語と異なり強く長く発音される部分（音節）と弱く短く発音される部分（音節）で構成されます。さらに，強く長く発音される部分と次に強く長く発音される部分までは，時間的にほぼ等しくなろうとする傾向があります（Unit 2）。例5のaからeの長さが，強く長く発音される部分の間に入る弱く短く発音される部分（音節）の数に関係なくほぼ等しい時間で発音される傾向があります。従って，強く長く発音される部分の間にある弱く短く発音される部分の数が増加するにつれて，弱く短く発音される部分の発音はより弱く，より短くなります。このような英語の音声特徴をよく認識した上で，英語を聞いたり話したりすることはとても重要なことです。

例6　College students visit the website to register for the courses.
　　　●(•)　　●(•)　　●(•)　•　●(•)　•　●(•)(•)　•　•　●　(•)
　　　|← a →|← b →|← c →|← d →|←　　e　　→|

5　light と right とライト

日本人は，英語を聞く時にも話す時にも l と r の区別に困難を感じている人が多いようです。練習のポイントは，日本語のライトと英語の light と right をしっかり区別することです。日本語のライトは，英語の light と right の音声特徴をある程度共有しているとも考えられます。具体的には，英語の [l] は，語頭にある場合には，舌の先をしっかりと上の歯茎につけて発音します。一方，英語の [r] は，舌先を丸めて口の中の奥の方へ持っていってから（巻き舌と言われている）発音します。従って，[r] は暗くこもったような音声になり [l] とはかなり音質の異なった音声になります。上手く巻き舌ができない場合には，英語の write を練習してください。本来英語の [w] は，唇をよく丸めて発音します。練習のためには，発音しない（黙字）w を唇をとがらせて発音するウのように発音し，ウライトのように発音することから練習してみてください。慣れてきたら，ウの音声は出さずにウの発音のかまえだけをして write を発音するようにしましょう。このように発音すると，巻き舌が自然にできる上に [r] 特有の暗くこもった音質も出てきます。最後に日本語のライ

トの音声特徴について考えてみます。日本語のラの発音は，語によってまた人によって異なりますが，舌の先が上の歯茎の少し後ろのところに触れたり触れなかったりして発音する傾向があります。触れれば [l] のように，触れなければ [r] のように聞こえてしまします。このような日本語の音声特徴のために，英語の [r] と [l] の区別が難しくなってしまうのです（Unit 18）。

6　語の位置の違いによる発音の違い

英語の発音の中には，語の初め（語頭），終わり（語末）そして語頭と語尾の間（語中）によって発音が異なるものがあります（Unit 4）。teach, system, cat に含まれる t の発音は，teach の場合口から勢いよく息をはき出しながら発音し，system では通常の t の発音をし，cat の場合には舌先を上の歯茎につけたままにして発音を終るか，舌先を上の歯茎から離す場合とても弱く息を出すようにすると英語らしい発音ができます。同じような発音の特徴は，people, happy, help; key, taking, look のような語に含まれる p, k の発音にも見られます。

7　強い発音と弱い発音

機能語と呼ばれる語は，文の中では発音の仕方が変化します。例えば，イギリスの代表的な食べ物である fish and chips は，and の発音が，ンのように弱く・短くなりフィシュンチップスのように発音されます。この発音をフィシュアン（ド）チップスと発音すると，特定の料理名ではなく魚とチップスという意味になります。実際に，英国のレストランでフィシュアンドチップスと発音しても，レストランで外国人が発音しているという状況判断から，魚とチップスと解釈される可能性は少ないのでそれほど心配することはないでしょう。発音の違いによって意味解釈が異なる同様な例としては，bread and butter が上げられます。ブレッドンバターはバターを塗ったパン，ブレッドアンドバターはパンとバターを示します。Rock'n'Roll も同じようにロックンロールと発音されます。このように機能語には，強く長く発音される強形と弱く短く発音される弱形の発音があります。and では，アンドが強形，アンヤン等が弱形になります。機能語は強形よりも弱形で発音されることがはるかに多いので，英語を聞き，話すためには，弱形をよく聞いて同じように発音できるように練習することが大切です。

Unit 1 で学んだように，基本的に強く発音される内容語（名詞，動詞，形容詞，副詞など）と弱く発音される機能語（代名詞，冠詞，接続詞，前置詞など）によって文のリズムが構成されます。Do の例では，強形は Do come right now! のように動詞を強める時，弱形は Do you come with me? のように疑問文等に現れます（Unit 12 参照）。

8　二語連続する場合の発音の変化

語が文の中に使用されると，その語本来の発音が変化することがあります。このような音声の変化は語と語が連続する時の最初の語の語末と次に来る語の語頭に関してよく現れます。good day（Unit 5）の場合には，good の語末の d の発音と次の語 day の語頭の d の発音が同じなので，語末の d の発音の際に息を吐き出さないでためておいた状態で語頭の d の発音に移ります。そう

することによって，グッドディのような発音から英語らしいグッディのような発音に変化します。good job (Unit 6) の場合も，同様な要領で発音すると，グッドジョブのような発音から英語らしいグッジョブのような発音に変化します。ただし，job の発音を英語らしくするには，語末の b を発音する時に，上と下の唇を合わせたままにして，息を吐き出さないようにするとよいでしょう。

　二語が連続する場合に，初めの語の語末と次に来る語の語頭の発音が連続して発音されることがあります。例としては, kick off (Unit 7) や clear up (Unit 8) 等があります。それぞれ，キックオフ，クリアーアップのような発音が，キッコフ，クリアラップのような発音に変化します。come on in (Unit 9) の場合にも，同様な変化がみられ，カムオンインのような発音から，カモニンのような発音になります。

　二語が連続する場合に，初めの語の語末と次に来る語の語頭の発音にいろいろと変化が見られることがあります。get you (Unit 10) の場合には，ゲットユーというよりは，ゲッチューのようになります。nice shot (Unit 11) の場合には，ナイスのスは，次にくるショットの発音の影響を受けてシュのように変化します。その結果ナイショットのように発音しますが，ポイントとしては，ナイショットのショの部分がナイスのスとショットのショの部分とが合わさったものであることを考えて長めに発音することです。さらに，nice shot の t の発音は舌先を上の歯茎につけたままにして発音を終るか，舌先を上の歯茎から離す場合とても弱く息を出すようにすると英語らしい発音になります。

　二語が連続する場合に，初めの語の語末が次に来る語の語頭の発音の影響を受けて発音されることがあります。例としては，of course (Unit 17) があり，オブコースではなく，オフコースのように発音されます。これは，次に来る語の語頭の音声 k が無声音であるという特徴によって，初めの語の語末の音声特徴が有声 v から無声 f へと変化することによって起こる音声現象です。同様な例は，have to にも見られる現象で，ハブトゥのような発音ではなくハフトゥのような発音になります。

　二語が連続する場合に，初めの語が次に来る語の影響を受けて発音されることがあります。例としては，can に not がついて否定され can't になると，通常 can は，弱く短く発音されますが，can't は強く長く発音されます (Unit 13)。二語が連続する場合に，次に来る語の発音が部分的になることもあります。例としては, You've (Unit 14) があり，ユーハブ (You have) ではなく，ユーブ（ブは v の発音を示す）のように発音します。

9　さまざまな発音事情

　コミュニケーションに大切な数量表現をしっかり聞き，発音できるように，小数点 (42. 195; Unit 19) や年号 (in 2008; Unit 20) なども練習してください。また，日本語的に発音している英語もしっかりと英語として発音するようにします。例としては，towel や major があり，タオル，メジャーのような発音から，タゥアル，メイジャーのような発音になるよう練習してください (Units 21&22)。

　アメリカ英語(AE)とイギリス英語(BE)の発音の違いについても学んでおきましょう。例としては，water や want to go 等があります (Units 23&24)。water の発音が BE ではウォーターのように発音されるのに対して，AE ではウォーダー，ウォーラーのように発音されることがあります。これは，AE では語に含まれる t の発音をする時の筋肉の緊張の度合いが弱まっていく時に生じる

音声現象です。同じような音声現象が日本語の表現「大丈夫だ」にも見られます。例えば，お酒に酔うにつれて，ダイジョウブダからライリョウブダのように変化していきます。want to go の発音が BE ではウォントゥゥゴゥのように発音されるのに対して，AE ではウォナゴーのように発音されることがあります。これは，want の語尾の t を発音しないこと，次に来る to も文の中では弱く短く発音されること，そして to が弱く短く発音されるとトゥのゥの発音がさらに弱くなり曖昧な発音になること等の結果生じる音声現象です。want の語尾の t を発音しないで舌先を上の歯茎につけておき，トゥのゥの発音がさらに弱くなり曖昧になった発音を連続すると，AE のウォナゴーのような発音になります。

くだけて話される英語やスピードが速く話される英語でも発音が変化することがあります。what time is it now? がホワットタイムではなく，ワッタイムのように聞こえたりする場合です（Unit 15）。また，文の意味を正確に把握するには，接続詞の発音にも気をつけましょう。例として，and や but 等（Unit 16）があり，アンド，バットのような発音から，弱く速く発音されるァン，バッ（ト）等の発音ができるように練習します。

10　英語らしい発音を身につける練習法

1．聞いた英語を文法や背景知識など英語と日本語の違いについての知識を総動員して意味のある英語として聞き取りましょう。
2．英語で書けない部分は，カタカナなどを利用して聞こえた通りに表記しておきます。
3．書き取った英語と正しい英語と比較する。自分の知っている英語が書き取れていない場合には，自分の頭に存在している英語の音声と実際に聞き取ろうとしている英語の音声とにズレが生じていることが考えられます。
4．英語で書けない部分をカタカナや発音記号などを利用して聞こえた通りに表記しておいたものと正しい英語をよく比較・検討しましょう。多くの場合には，ここまでに学んだ音声特徴で聞き誤りの原因が理解できると思われますが，中にはその理由が理解できないものもあるかもしれません。そのような音声特徴は，もっと英語力がついてから学ぶことにして，今は聞こえた通りに発音する練習をしておきましょう。
5．大切なことは，聞き取りがよくできなかった発音をよく練習した上で，できる限り聞こえてくる英語と同じような発音になるまで練習することです。そこで役立つ方法がシャドーイング（shadowing）です。これは，聞こえてくる英語を瞬時にリピートする方法です。できる限りあらゆる音声特徴を模倣してリピートしましょう。
6．音声特徴を目や耳で確かめながら学習する時に音声分析機器を利用することも一案です。フリーソフトの Praat（プラート）などを使用して，英語音声の特徴を分析しながら練習するのも効果的に英語の音声を理解し身につける良い方法です。
http://www.fon.hum.uva.nl/praat/download_win.html

英語を聞き，話すための基礎的な力（初級）をつけ，次のステップ（中級・上級）へと進み，グローバル社会でそれぞれの仕事・研究ができるようになることを期待しています。

主　幹	高橋　寿夫
執筆者	伊與田　洋之
	神室　芽久美
	工藤　和也
	笹井　悦子
	高橋　寿夫
	樽井　武
	原田　洋子
	藤本　恵子
	松村　優子

著作権法上、無断複写・複製は禁じられています。

Power-Up English <Pre-Intermediate>　　　　　　　　　　　　　　[B-772]
総合英語パワーアップ＜初級編＞

1　刷	2015年2月12日
10　刷	2024年3月29日

著　者	JACETリスニング研究会
発行者	南雲　一範　Kazunori Nagumo
発行所	株式会社　南雲堂
	〒162-0801　東京都新宿区山吹町361
	NAN'UN-DO CO., Ltd.
	361 Yamabuki-cho, Shinjuku-ku, Tokyo 162-0801, Japan
	振替口座：00160-0-46863
	TEL：03-3268-2311（代表）／FAX：03-3269-2486
	編集者　加藤　敦
組　版	柴崎　利恵
イラスト	MAKOTO
装　丁	Nスタジオ
検　印	省略
コード	ISBN978-4-523-17772-2　C0082

Printed in Japan

E-mail　　nanundo@post.email.ne.jp
URL　　　https://www.nanun-do.co.jp/